Also by Liza Donnelly and Michael Maslin

Call Me When You Reach Nirvana
Husbands and Wives

Edited by Liza Donnelly and Michael Maslin

Fathers and Sons

Also by Liza Donnelly

Sex and Sensibility: Ten Women Examine the Lunacy of Modern Love . . . in 200 Cartoons
Funny Ladies: The New Yorker's Greatest Women Cartoonists and Their Cartoons
Mothers and Daughters

Also by Michael Maslin

The More the Merrier
The Gang's All Here!
The Crowd Goes Wild
Mixed Company

Cartoon Marriage

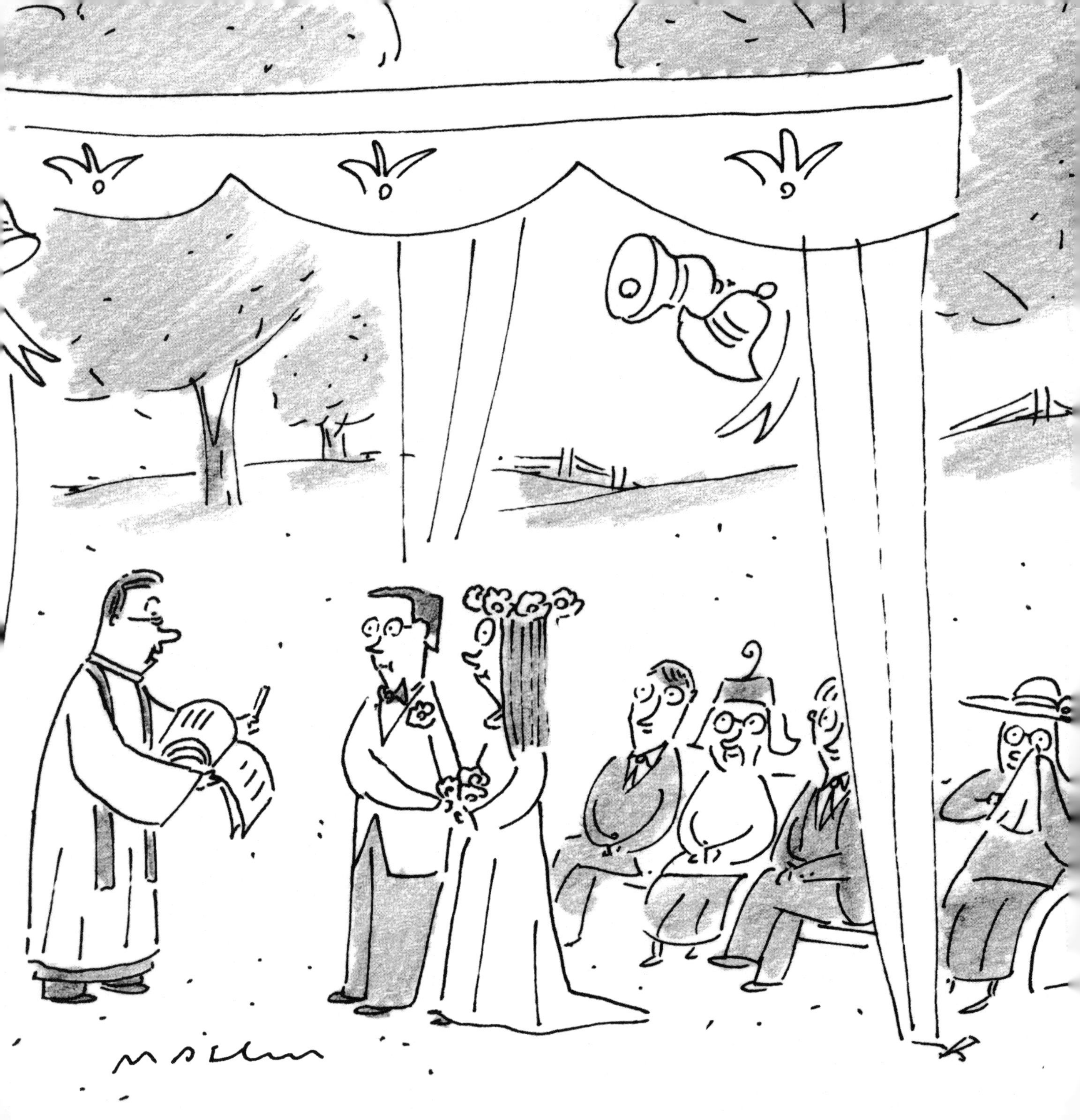

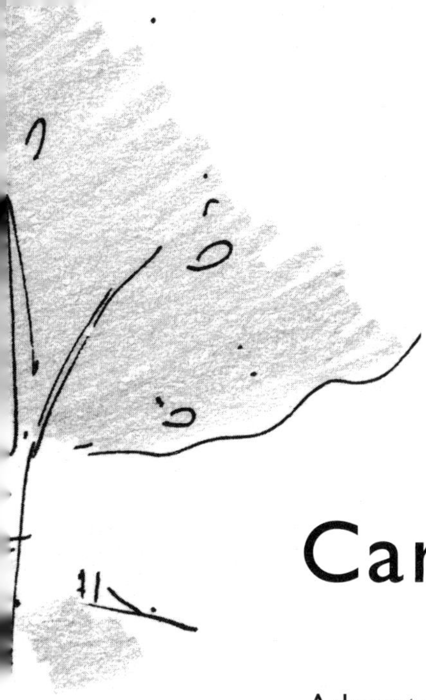

Cartoon Marriage

Adventures in Love and Matrimony

by *The New Yorker*'s Cartooning Couple

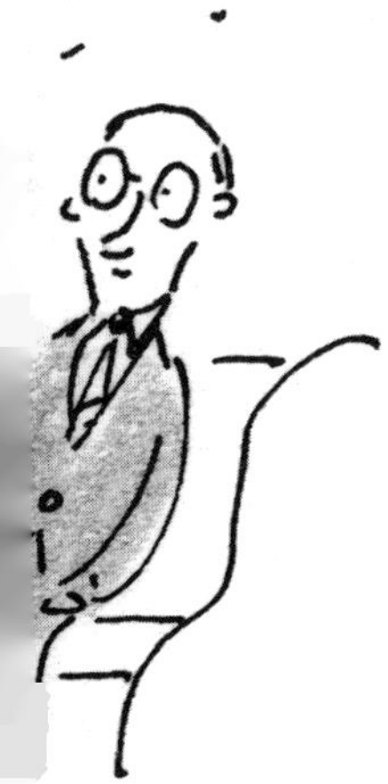

Liza Donnelly and

Michael Maslin

Random House · New York

Published in the United States by Random House,
an imprint of The Random House Publishing Group,
a division of Random House, Inc., New York.

RANDOM HOUSE and colophon are registered
trademarks of Random House, Inc.

Cartoons on pages 29, 38, 50, 55, 66, 74, 88, 90, 92, 93, 94, 107, 142, 159, 205,
208, 220, 224, 238, 258, 260, 270, 274, and 276 are copyright © Liza Donnelly,
The New Yorker Collection, 2008. Cartoons on pages 7, 11, 20, 26, 52, 67, 69, 81,
94, 104, 119, 124, 129, 134, 161, 168, 189, 197, 211, 214, 215, 223, 226, 234, 240, 247,
261, 269, 271, and 273 are copyright © Michael Maslin, The New Yorker Collection, 2008.

LIBRARY OF CONGRESS CATALOGING-IN-PUBLICATION DATA

Donnelly, Liza.
Cartoon marriage: adventures in love and matrimony by the
New Yorker's cartooning couple / Liza Donnelly and Michael Maslin.
p. cm.
ISBN 978-1-4000-6808-1
1. Marriage—Caricatures and cartoons.   2. Love—Caricatures and cartoons.
3. American wit and humor, Pictorial.   I. Maslin, Michael.
II. New Yorker (New York, N.Y.: 1925).   III. Title.
NC1429.D565A4 2009   741.5'6973—dc22   2008028993

Printed in the United States of America on acid-free paper

www.atrandom.com

1 2 3 4 5 6 7 8 9

FIRST EDITION

Book design by Dana Leigh Blanchette

To our daughters, Ella and Gretchen

Contents

Here's the Story of Us . . .

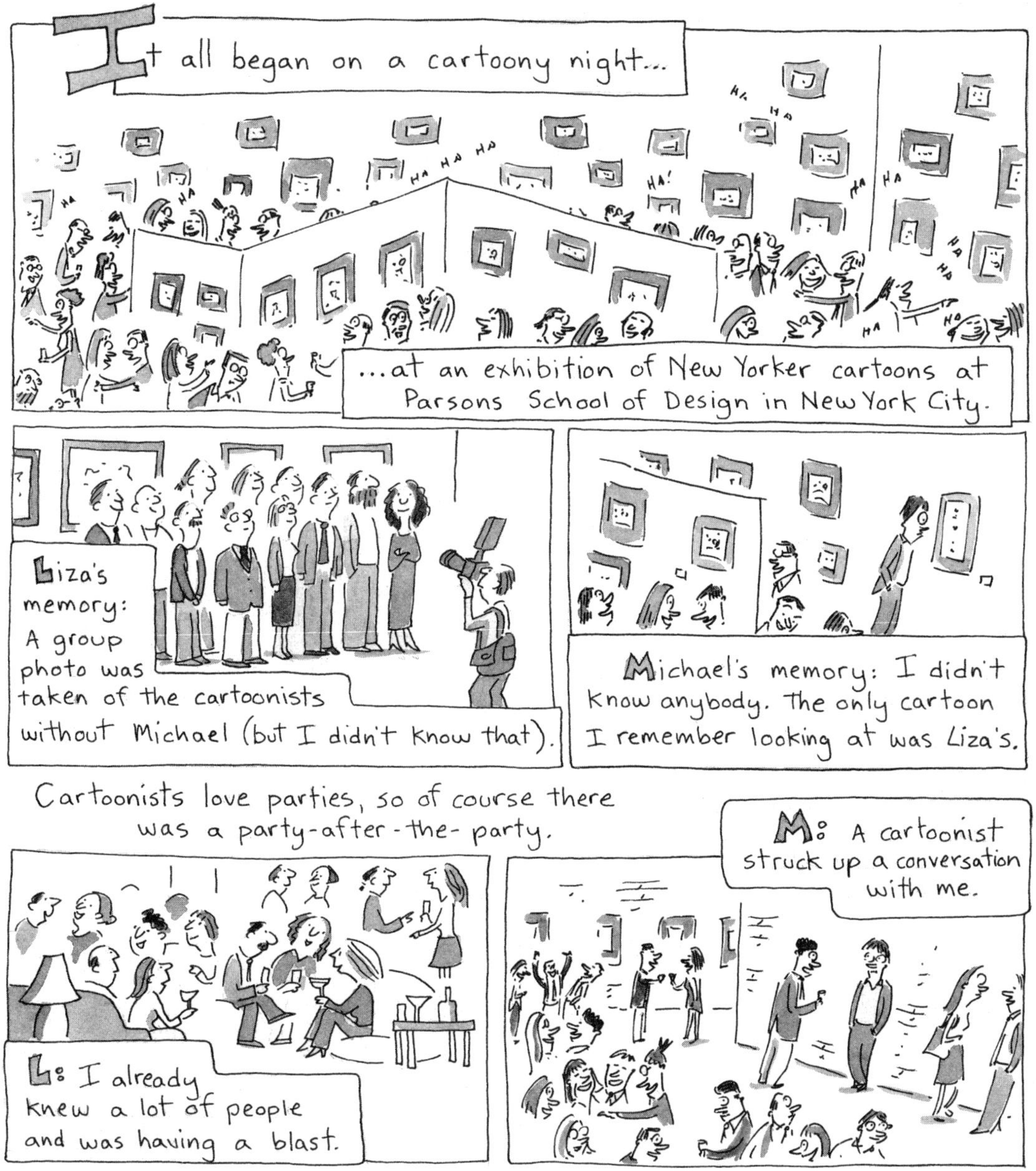
It all began on a cartoony night...
...at an exhibition of New Yorker cartoons at Parsons School of Design in New York City.
Liza's memory: A group photo was taken of the cartoonists without Michael (but I didn't know that).
Michael's memory: I didn't know anybody. The only cartoon I remember looking at was Liza's.
Cartoonists love parties, so of course there was a party-after-the-party.
L: I already knew a lot of people and was having a blast.
M: A cartoonist struck up a conversation with me.

We shook hands in a sea of cartoonists.

cartoonists

cartoonist

cartoonist

M: Suddenly, I was introduced to a bunch of cartoonists. A young woman stepped up, arm extended, and shook my hand. "Hi! I'm Liza Donnelly."

L: I now remember meeting Michael, but the moment was fleeting and I immediately forgot it.

A few weeks later, the annual New Yorker anniversary party was held at the Pierre Hotel.

M: I watched Liza dance by.

Then, of course, the party-after-the-party. This time at Liza's apartment on W. 79th St.

Dick Cline

Roz Chast

Michael

Peter Steiner

Jack Ziegler

Mick Stevens

A very small apartment full of funny people.

L: As he was leaving, I gave Michael a poster from a cartoon exhibit...

...I was intrigued by his interest in all things cartoony. He left happy.

Two years later, we were in different places.

Michael was in upstate N.Y.

Liza was about to quit cartoons.

Then, another New Yorker anniversary party. At the after-party, we talked for the first time, and the subject of Thurber came up.

"Thurber" was James Thurber, the late, great humorist and cartoonist.

L: I liked the simplicity of Thurber's art and had traced it at age 10... his cartoon women scared me, though.

We had both come to be Thurber fanatics in different ways. His approach to cartooning —and humor— was to become our bond.

THE FIRST TIME I SAW A THURBER DRAWING I JUMPED OUT OF MY SHOES. AMAZING BOOK: THE THURBER CARNIVAL

About a week later, we met on the steps of the Armory.

What do those raised eyebrows mean?

Do I like this guy? Oh, right. This is professional.

The Armory was full of great original art that was scheduled to be auctioned. Illustrations and cartoons. AND an original Thurber.

L: I really wanted to bid on the Thurber but to do so we would have to bid together. We barely knew each other!

PILES AND PILES OF CARTOONS ON FOLDING TABLES

BARSOTTI
SOGLOW
ARNO
A THURBER
SAXON
G. PRICE

M: I was thinking more about Liza than cartoons and I wondered: Was Liza thinking more about cartoons or me?

After seeing all that art, we needed coffee.
So we went to a diner down the street. Over lunch, the conversation turned from Thurber and cartoonists and The New Yorker...

COFFEE

... to us.

Cartoon Marriage

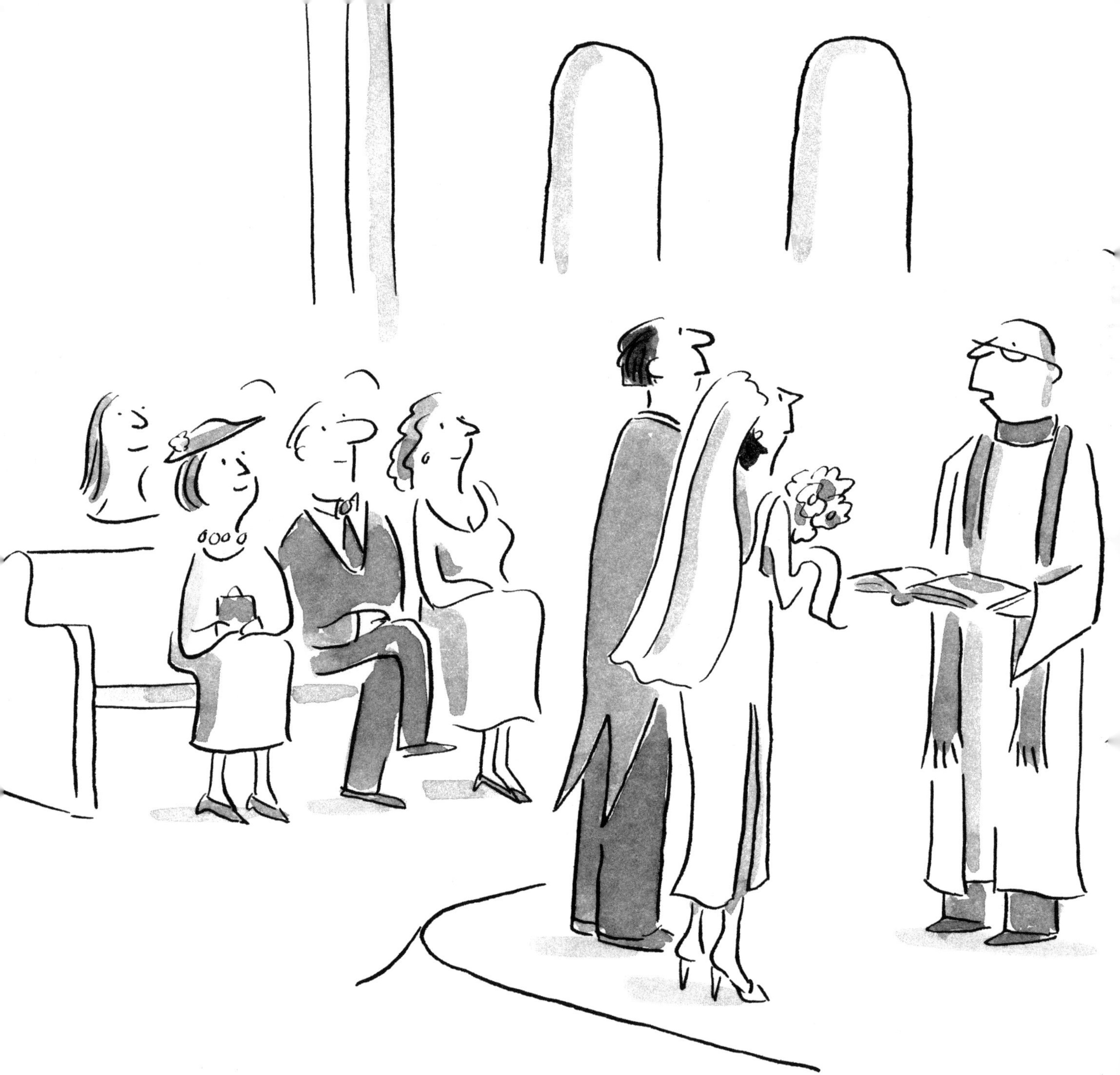

I Do?

You Should Have Told Me
That Before We Were Married.

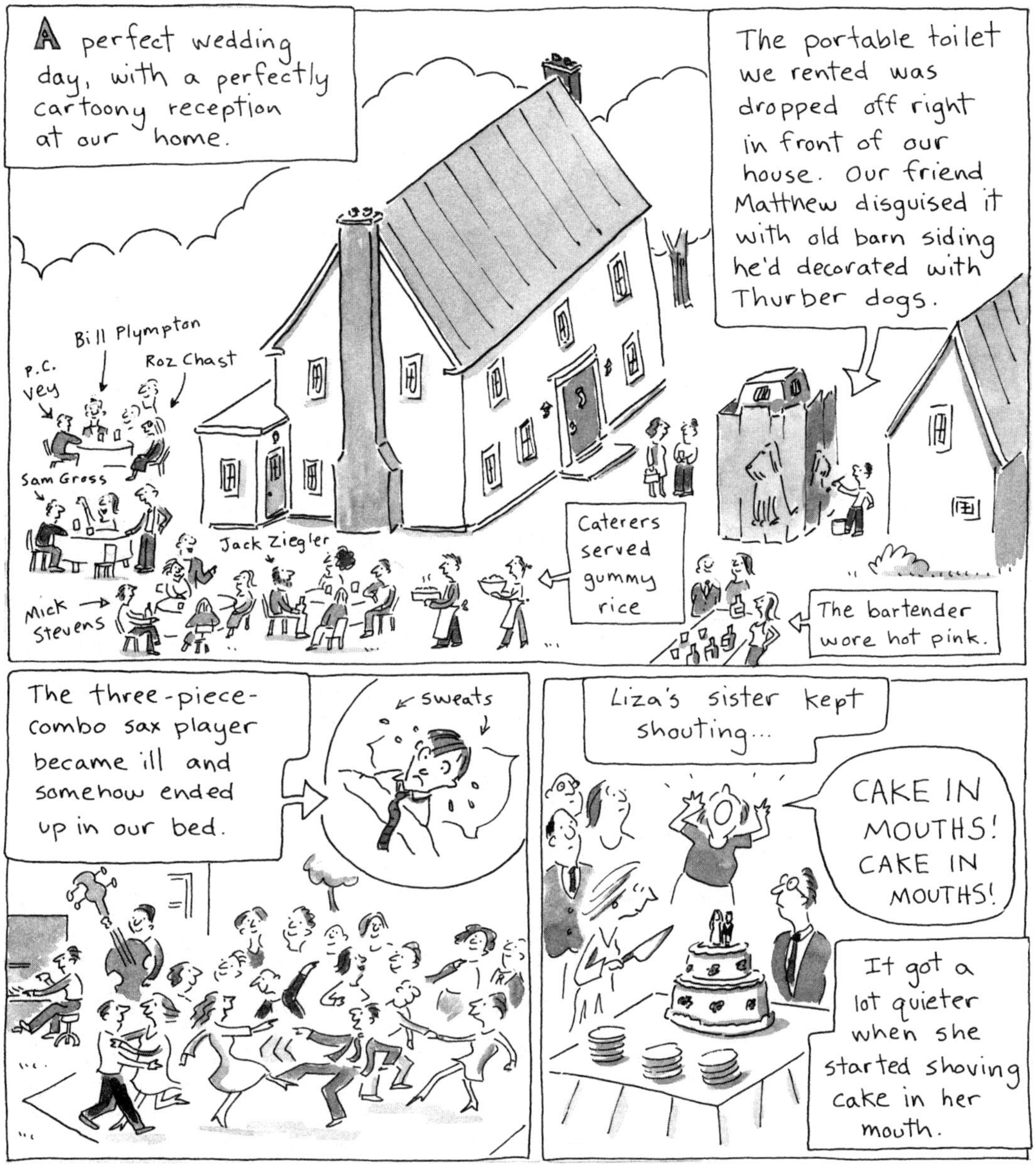
A perfect wedding day, with a perfectly cartoony reception at our home.
The portable toilet we rented was dropped off right in front of our house. Our friend Matthew disguised it with old barn siding he'd decorated with Thurber dogs.
Bill Plympton
P.C. Vey
Roz Chast
Sam Gross
Jack Ziegler
Mick Stevens
Caterers served gummy rice
The bartender wore hot pink.
The three-piece-combo sax player became ill and somehow ended up in our bed.
sweats
Liza's sister kept shouting...
CAKE IN MOUTHS! CAKE IN MOUTHS!
It got a lot quieter when she started shoving cake in her mouth.

"I could've sworn I just heard a commitment."

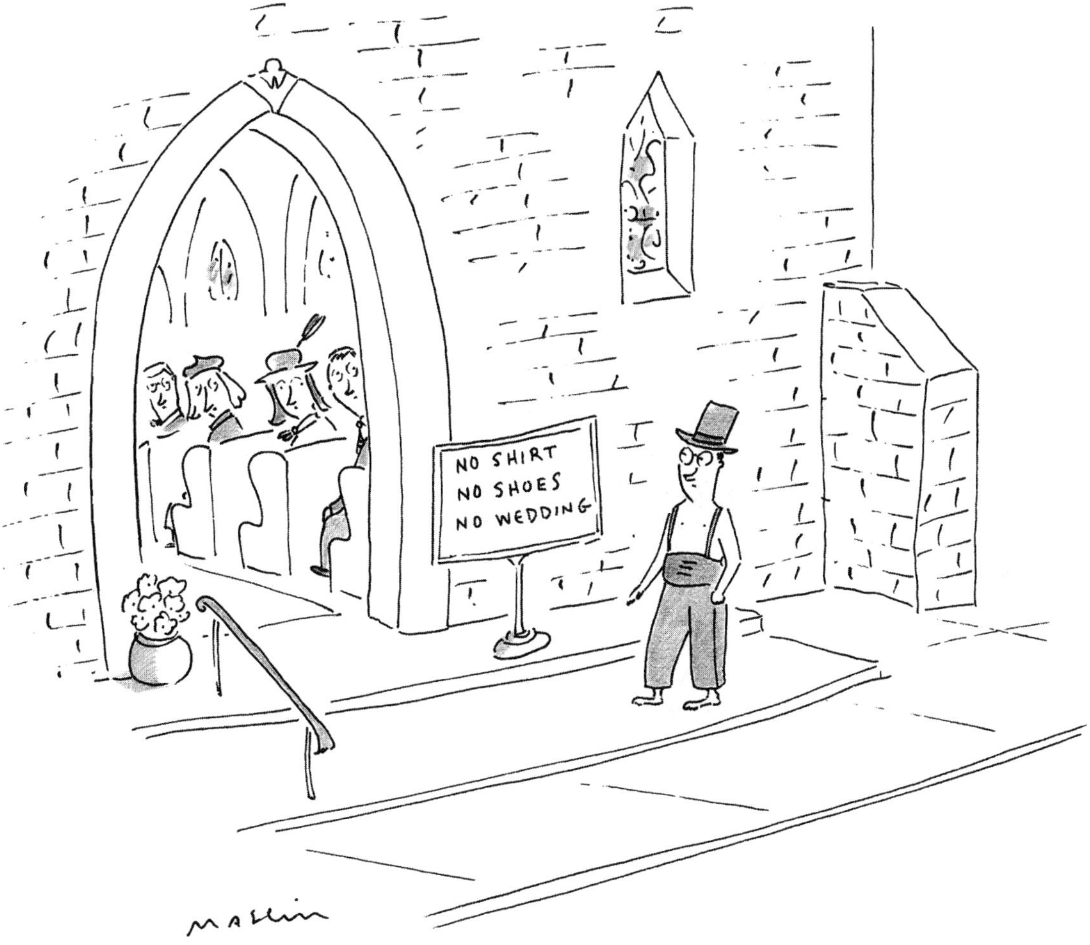
NO SHIRT
NO SHOES
NO WEDDING
MASLIN

"... And do you, Sally, take Jack to be
your husband until really, really pissed-off do you part?"

DONNELLY

"Marry me, Bridget—I want to spend at least a couple of
years of the rest of my life with you."

"*I've seen you in sickness and in health,
but never before knee-deep in a brook.*"

"Take your time, Mrs. Crimbly. Do you see the man who married you?"

11

"By the power vested in me, I now pronounce you husband versus wife."

"Remember when we first met and I was still finding myself and you were still finding yourself and you said you found yourself when you found me and I said I found myself when I found you? I lied."

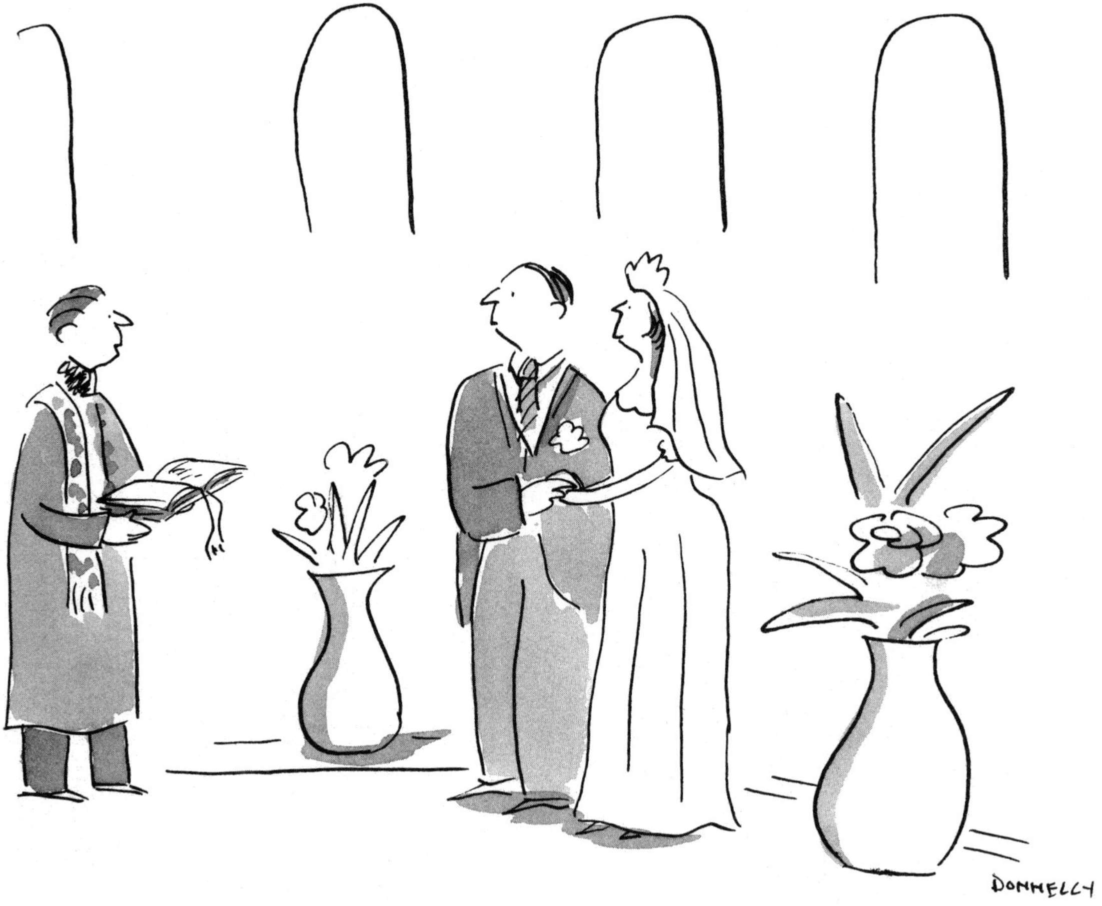
DONNELLY

*"Do you promise to love, honor, and always say,
'Who's there?' when she says, 'Knock-knock'?"*

"What do you take with your marriage?"

"You weren't this clingy before
we were married."

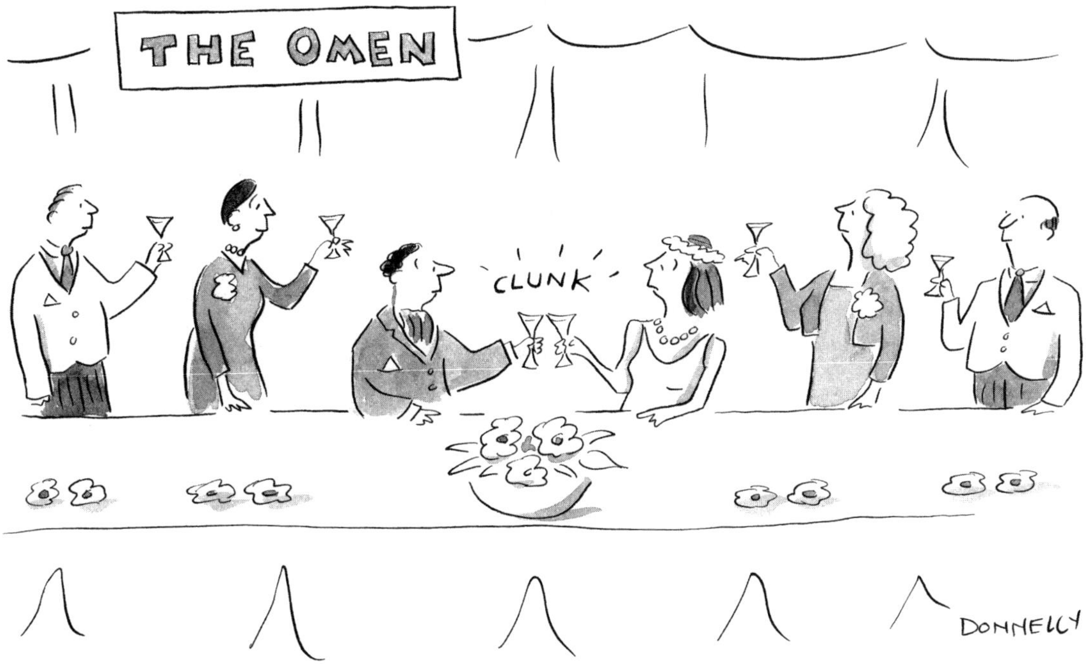
THE OMEN
CLUNK
DONNELLY

"O.K., O.K., so I'm wrong. Our marriage vows _are_ written in stone."

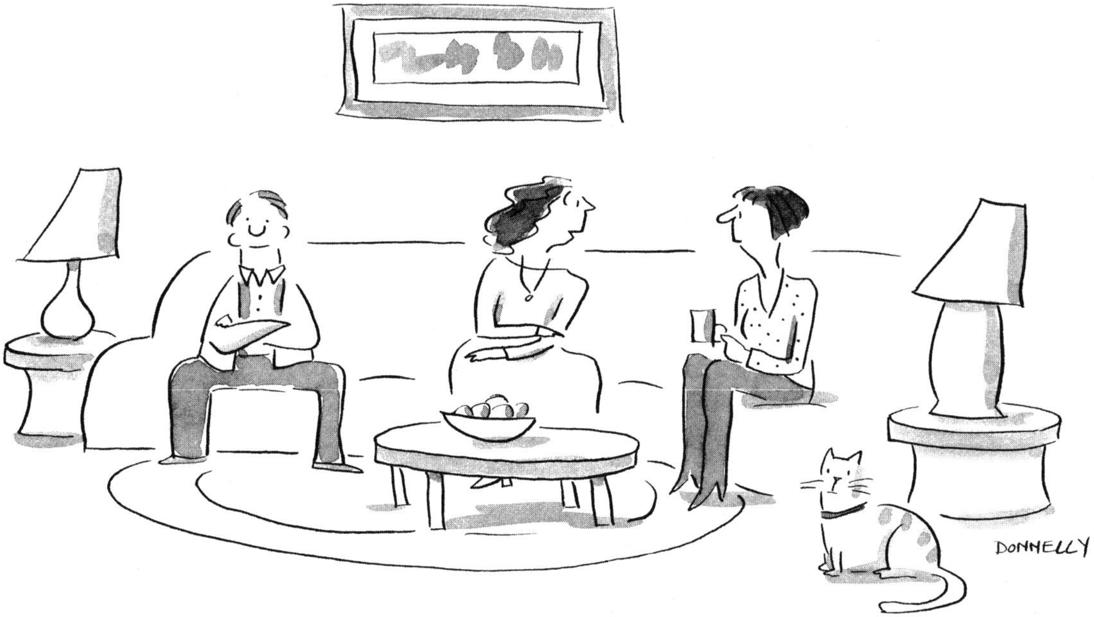
DONNELLY

"I married a blank slate."

"I'd give you the moon and stars, Felicia,
but I don't know where you'd put them."

"I love weddings. I'm going to have a bunch."

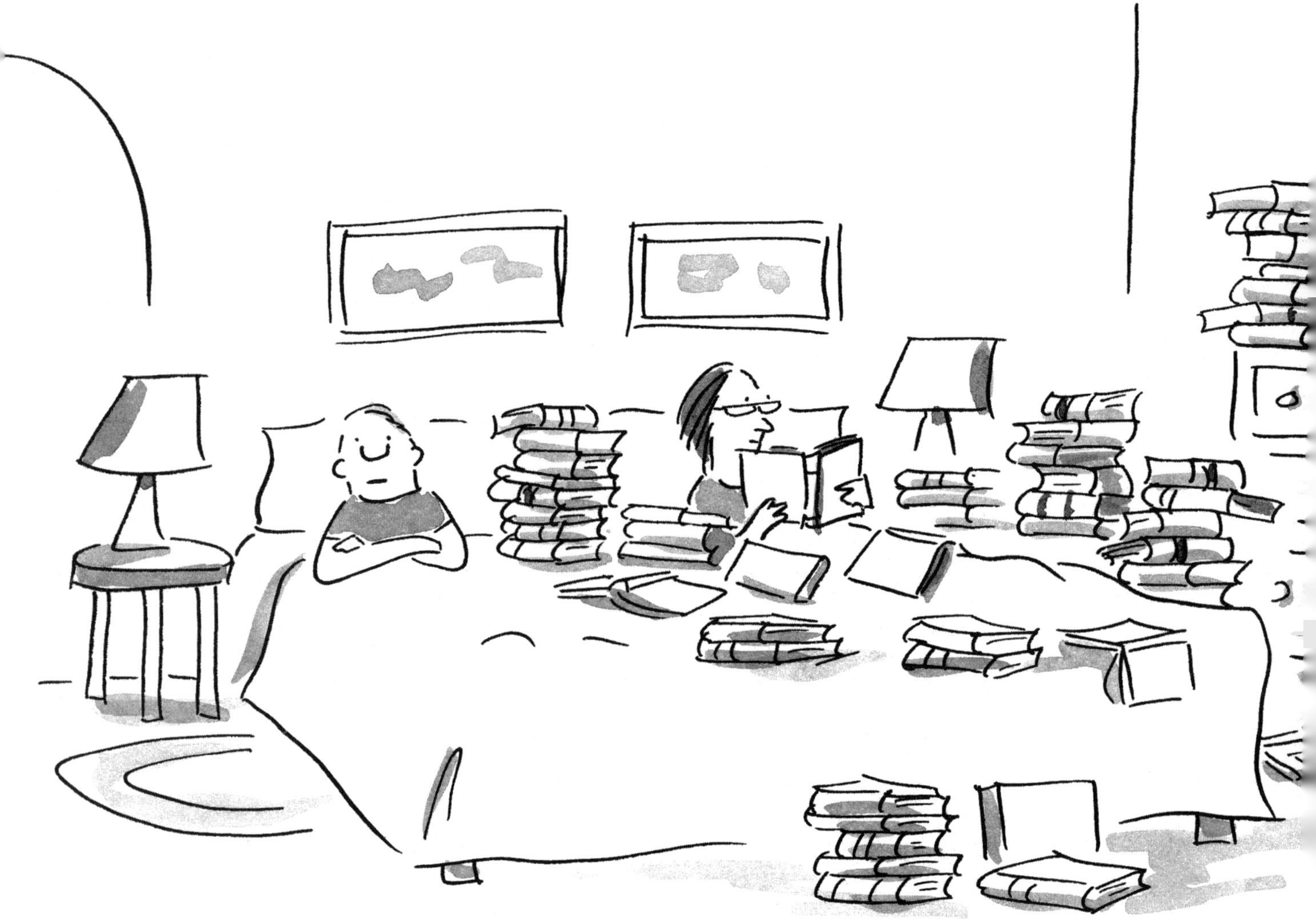

In Bed

Do You Want to Do That?

DONNELLY

Sure, there's a long, silly history of cartoonists drawing people asleep...

But if there's one thing cartoonists enjoy as much as drawing people asleep, it's drawing people awake...

...in bed.

Beds are a couple's battleground and/or playground.

Now, take two cartoonists married to each other, like us for instance, stick them in bed together...

.... and the result is

"Owen, look—the good-sex fairy."

"You've submitted an incorrect password.
Access denied."

"I don't get it, Molly—what's he
got that I don't have?"

"It won't work if I tell you what I want, because if I tell
you what I want I won't want it anymore."

"*Faster than a speeding bullet is right.*"

WOMEN WHO READ TOO MUCH
FICTION AND THE MEN WHO LOVE THEM

31

"I think it was better in rehearsal."

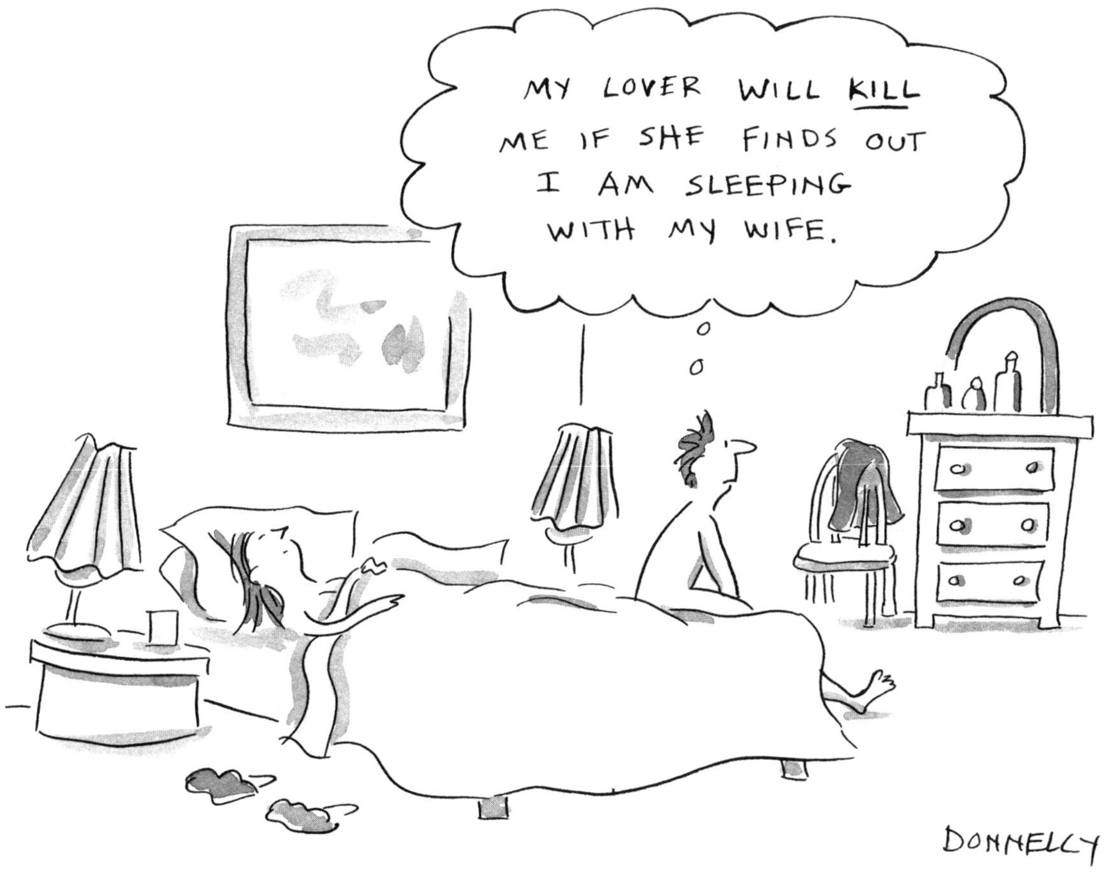
MY LOVER WILL KILL ME IF SHE FINDS OUT I AM SLEEPING WITH MY WIFE.
DONNELLY

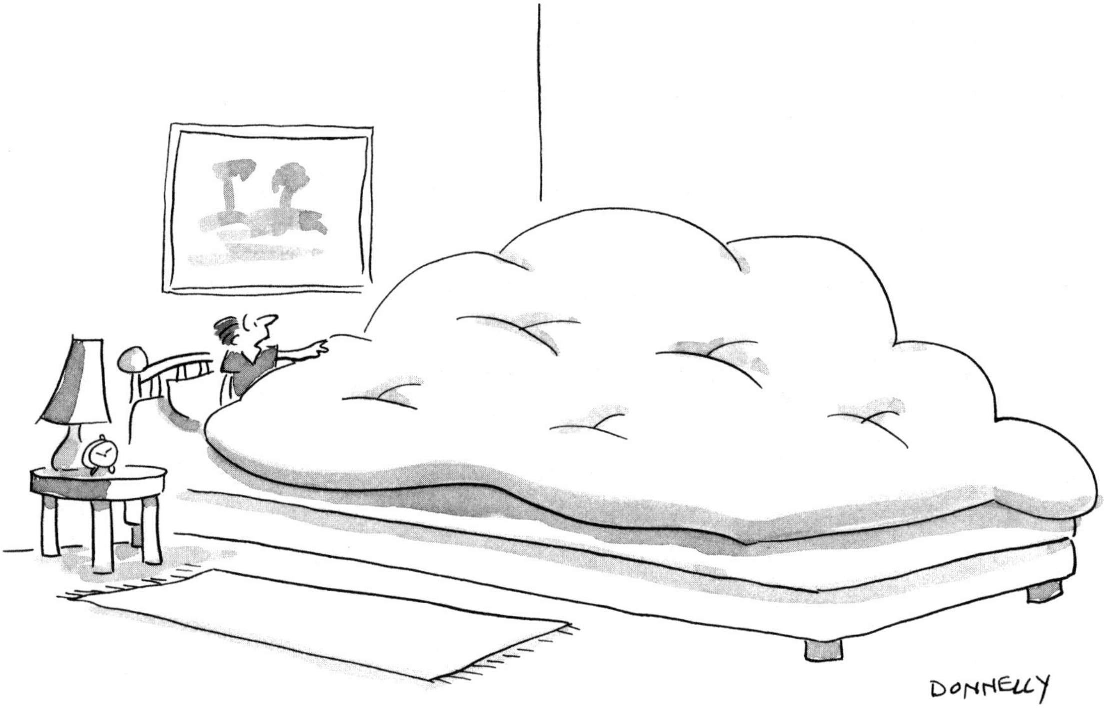
DONNELLY

"Louise? Are you in there?"

"Don't worry. I've performed this
procedure before."

"You're hogging the covers again,
over!"

"Push-button, rotary, cordless, or
cell phone sex tonight, sweetie?"

"So it's true. You really are all business."

"I love you for your funny."

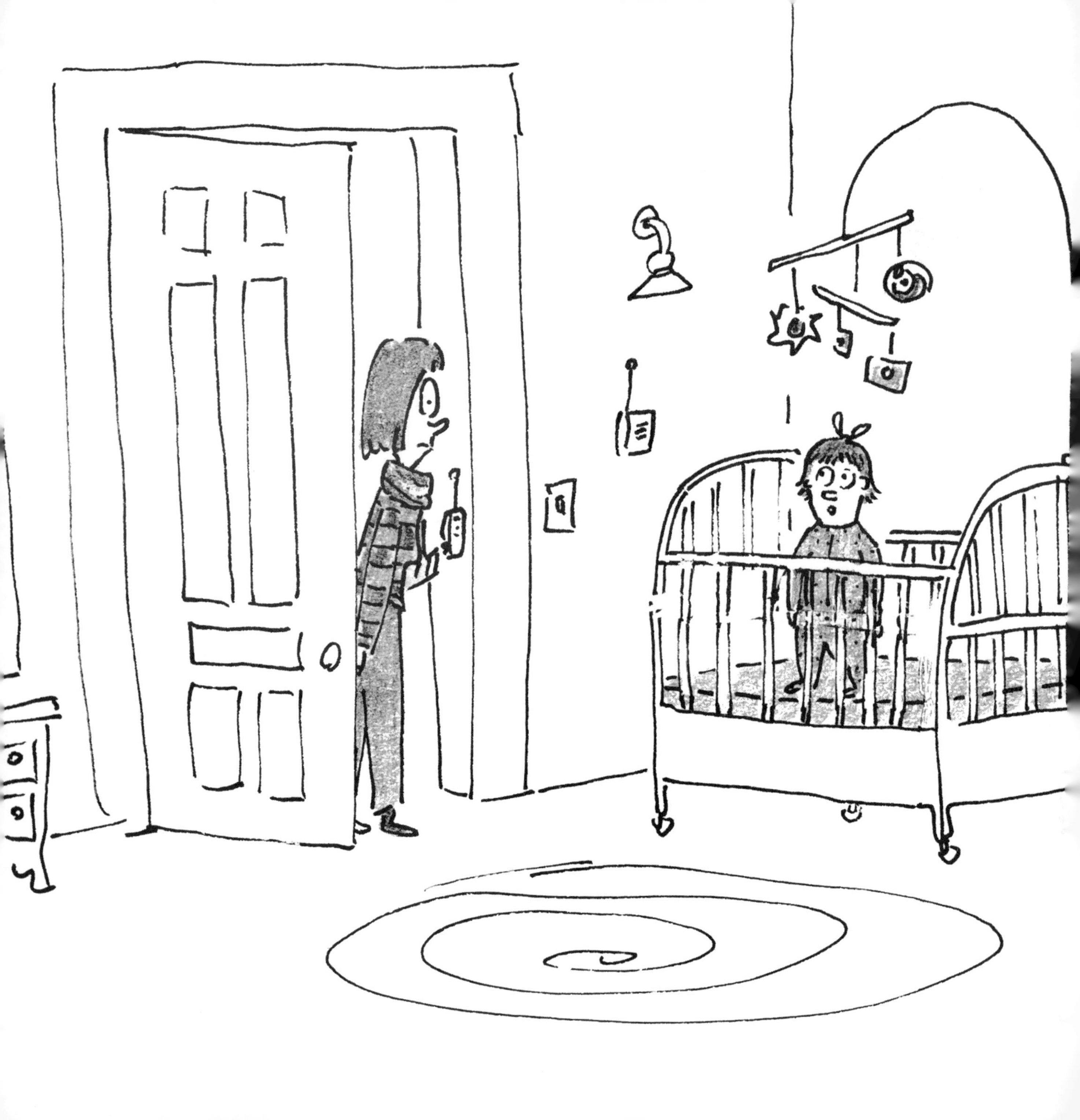

The Little Darlin's

What Were We Thinking?

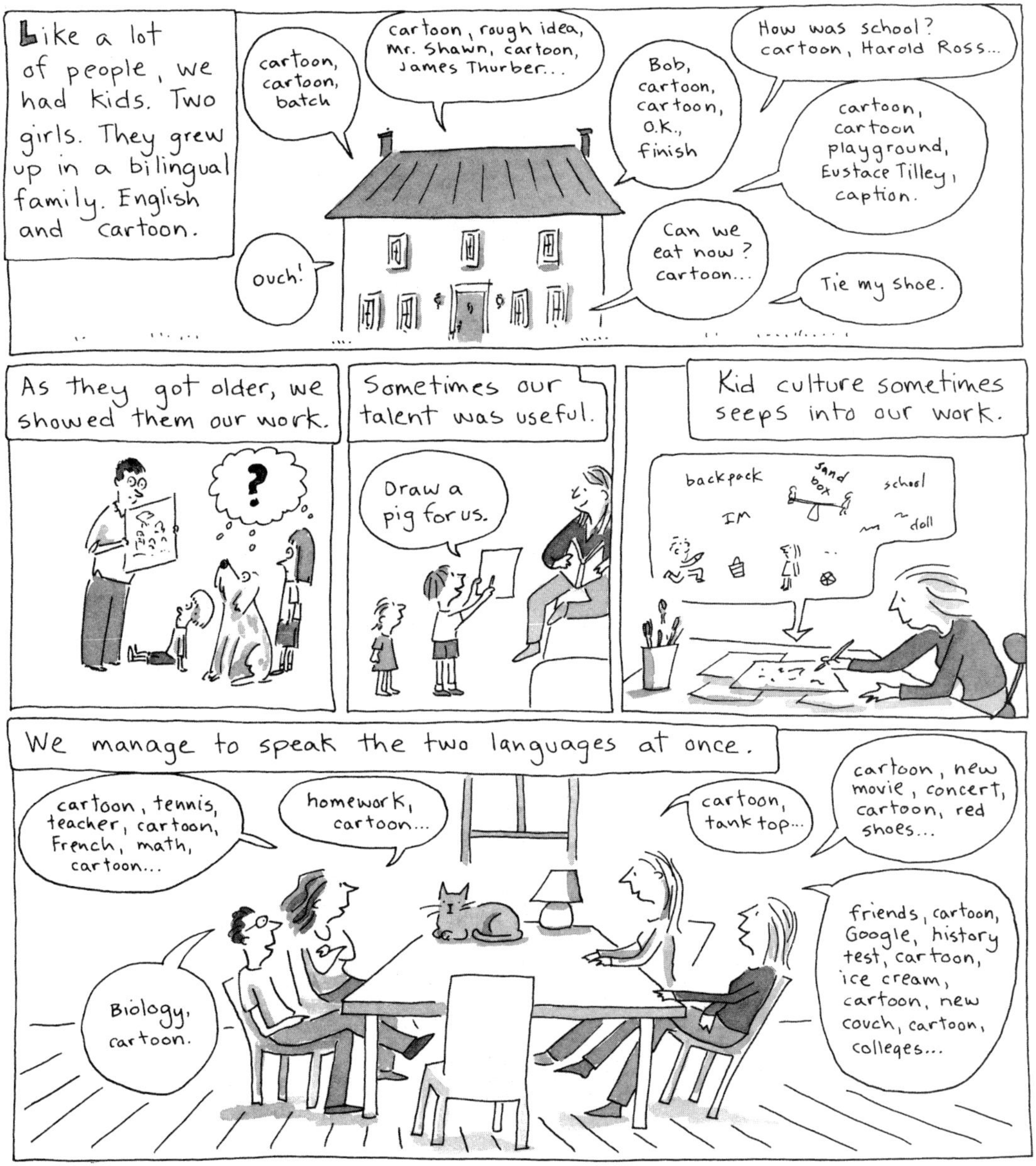
Like a lot of people, we had kids. Two girls. They grew up in a bilingual family. English and cartoon.
cartoon, cartoon, batch
cartoon, rough idea, Mr. Shawn, cartoon, James Thurber...
Bob, cartoon, cartoon, O.K., finish
How was school? cartoon, Harold Ross...
cartoon, cartoon playground, Eustace Tilley, caption.
ouch!
Can we eat now? cartoon...
Tie my shoe.
As they got older, we showed them our work.
Sometimes our talent was useful.
Draw a pig for us.
Kid culture sometimes seeps into our work.
backpack
sand box
school
IM
doll
We manage to speak the two languages at once.
cartoon, tennis, teacher, cartoon, French, math, cartoon...
homework, cartoon...
cartoon, tank top...
cartoon, new movie, concert, cartoon, red shoes...
friends, cartoon, Google, history test, cartoon, ice cream, cartoon, new couch, cartoon, colleges...
Biology, cartoon.

"Well, if you didn't want children, why did you marry me?"

"Will you still love us if we say 'no'?"

"*Effective immediately, I would like to begin calling you
'Dad' instead of 'Daddy,' and calling you 'Mom' instead of 'Mommy.'*"

"That'll look good on his college application."

"So if the baby monitor doesn't work,
you're suggesting I do what . . . scream?"

"Now that you're old and married, Mom, do you
miss coloring your hair green?"

"I'm staying together for the sake of my parents."

"Joey's made another wonderful clay paperweight,
and this one's for you."

"I don't have my homework, Miss Flynn—my parents forgot to do it."

"Dad says that what with all the advances in equality for women,
you can explain this fifty-seven-piece metric socket set
just as well as, if not better than, he can."

"Preschools? No, we thought
we'd better start looking at colleges."

"This is our son, Eddie. He's just graduated from school
and is entering a void this fall."

"We're already planning a sequel."

"Now that I'm a teenager, I know they expect moodiness
and distance from me, and I don't want to disappoint them."

"Sorry I'm late. My mom was
teaching me how to spit."

"You run along, Dad, and play with Mom."

"They're so cute at this stage."

"I liked it better when _I_ was your problem."

"Dad says it's all right with him if I watch TV
as long as it's not all right with you."

"Geez, Mom. I told her you wouldn't bite."

"I'll be out here until the
children are grown."

*"Amanda would like to issue her apology
to you in the form of a kiss on the cheek."*

"Now that our last is off to college,
could you tell me who the hell you are?"

"It's very, very important that you try very, very hard to remember where
you electronically transferred Mommy and Daddy's assets."

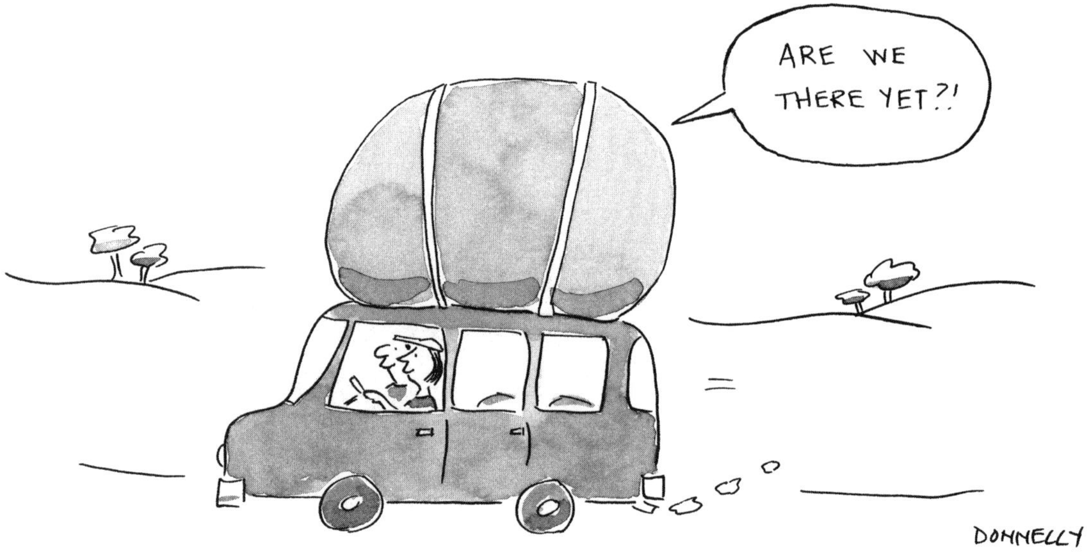
ARE WE THERE YET?!
DONNELLY

STRESS-FREE FAMILY VACATION

"I think he's finally asleep."

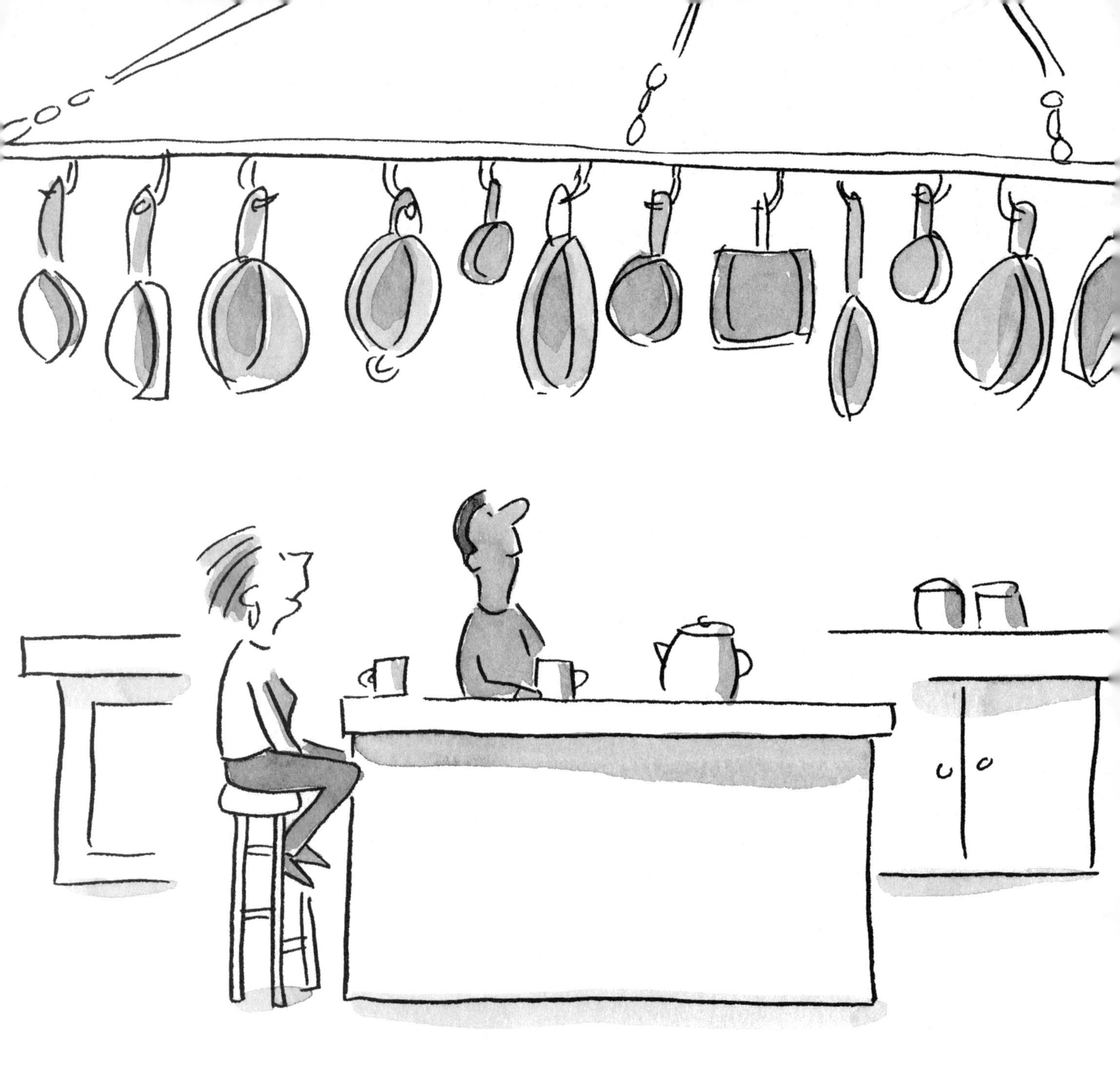

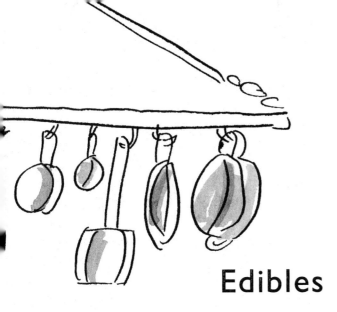

Edibles

I Really Love Your Meat Loaf,
But . . .

DONNELLY

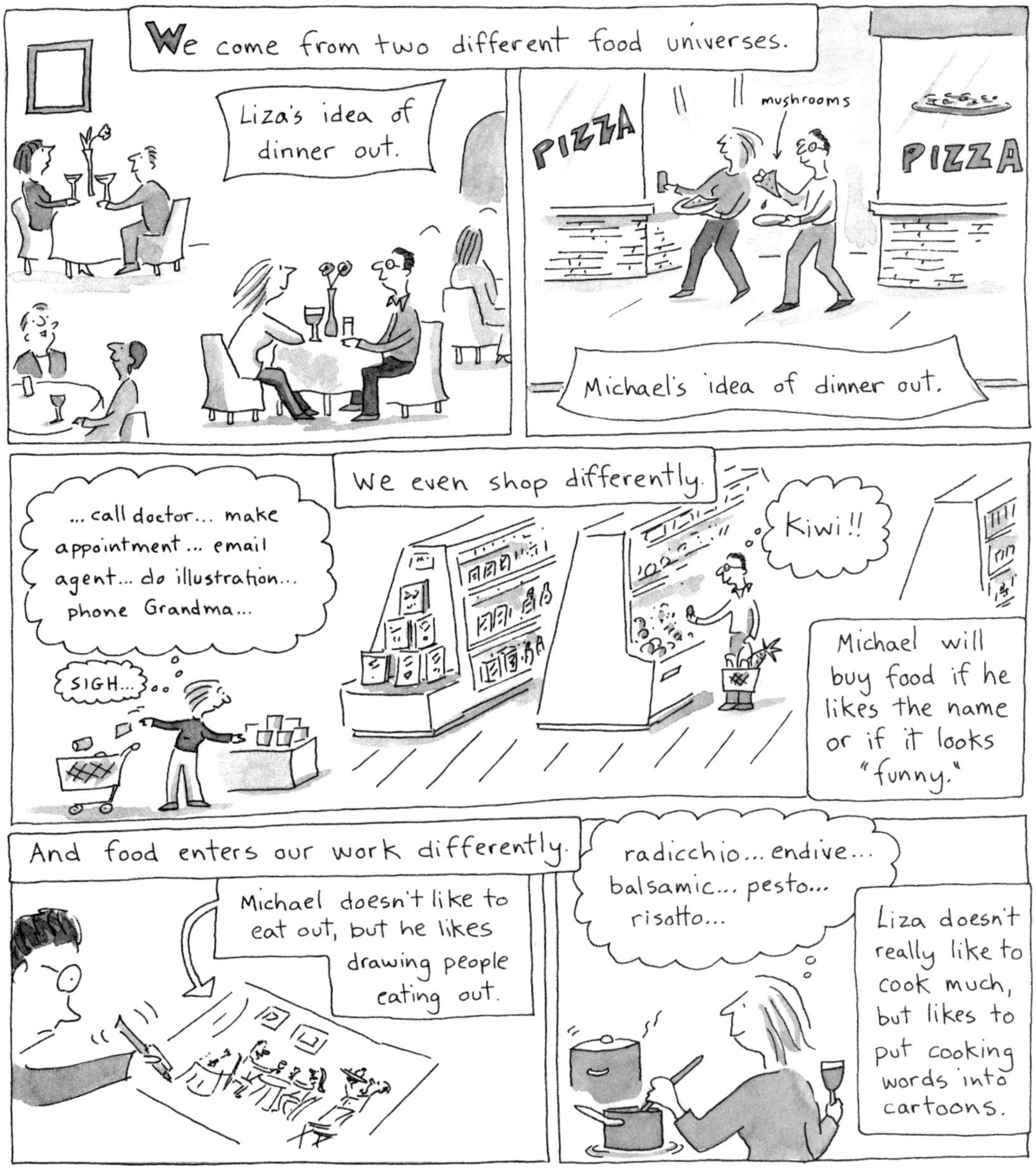
We come from two different food universes.
Liza's idea of dinner out.
PIZZA
mushrooms
PIZZA
Michael's idea of dinner out.
We even shop differently.
... call doctor... make appointment... email agent... do illustration... phone Grandma...
SIGH...
Kiwi!!
Michael will buy food if he likes the name or if it looks "funny."
And food enters our work differently.
Michael doesn't like to eat out, but he likes drawing people eating out.
radicchio... endive... balsamic... pesto... risotto...
Liza doesn't really like to cook much, but likes to put cooking words into cartoons.

"O.K., everybody, let's eat before the food gets dirty!"

"The food here's so-so, but the service is fabulous."

"Can she call you back? She's in the
middle of a tricky garlic rub."

"I was really hoping we could resolve this dispute
without resorting to a pie fight."

"Have you considered expressing
yourself through cooking?"

"He can be left alone for most of the day,
but I do have to be back to give him dinner."

"Do you think Jim and Julie are béarnaise, hollandaise, or bordelaise people?"

"And a side order of fries."

"I never cook.
That would be way too wife."

"Carl likes spending his summers grilling
one big hot dog instead of a lot of little ones."

"Do you want to eat first or wait until after our fight?"

"A scoop of butter almond on a sugar cone.
Ah, you'd better make that a double dip."

"Every skillet tells a story."

"I don't mind munching. Crunching, I mind."

"Some wine with your vest?"

"Can you recommend a wine? It's our first marriage."

"I feel like fooling around with radicchio."

"They ran out of hot dogs, so I got you
a tofu burger with sprouts."

"And when you said that my pesto was the best pesto you ever had
and could ever hope to have—was <u>that</u> a lie, too?"

"Hello? Risotto-crisis hotline?"

"Well, enough about us—let's talk about them."

"I'm sorry—I never should have offered you something I knew I couldn't deliver. There isn't any sprig of mint for your iced tea."

"Is that my crêpe or yours?"

"The crème brûlée is very, very bad today."

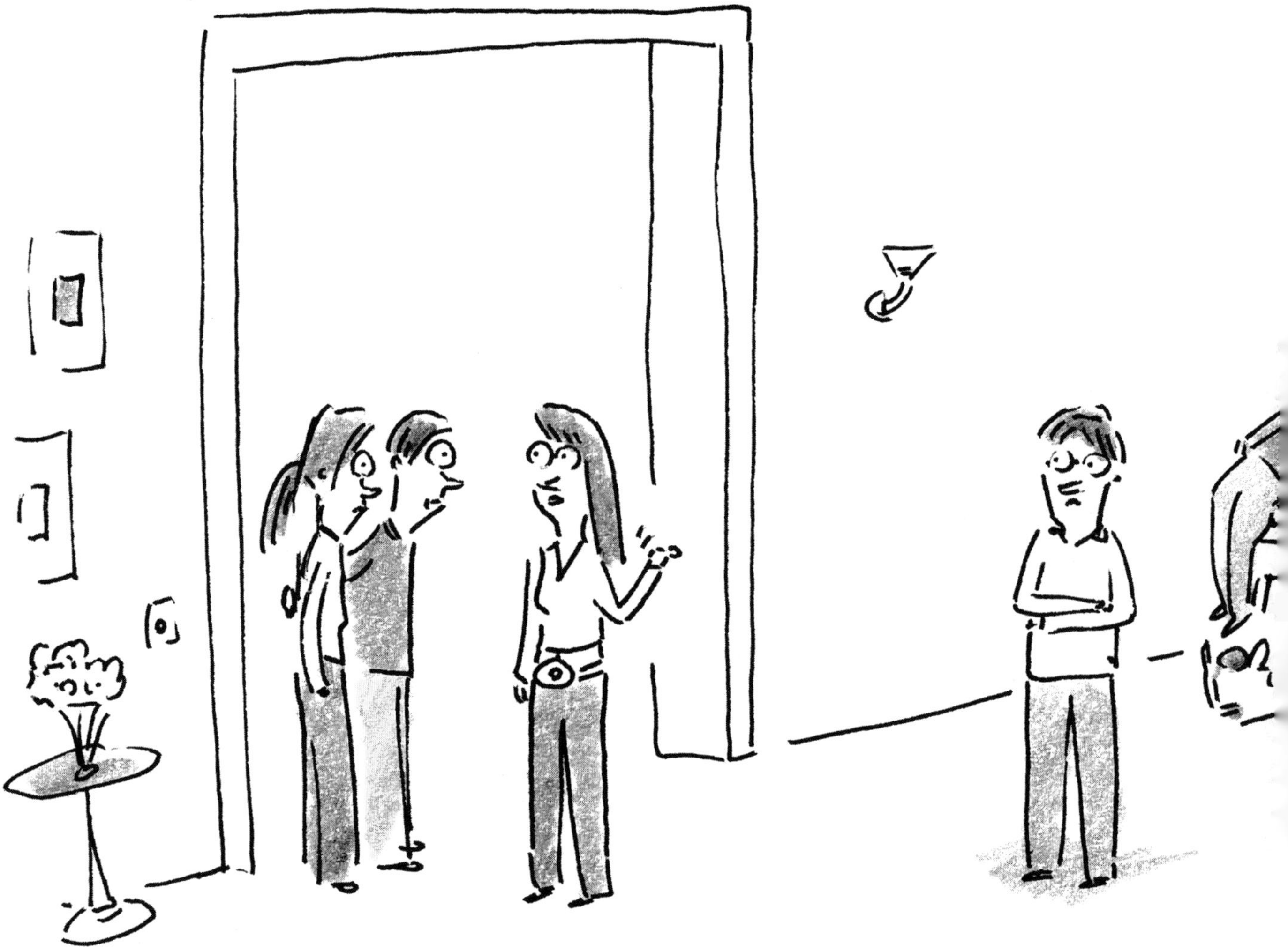

Ex-Whatevers

*Tell Me Everything That
I Don't Want to Know.*

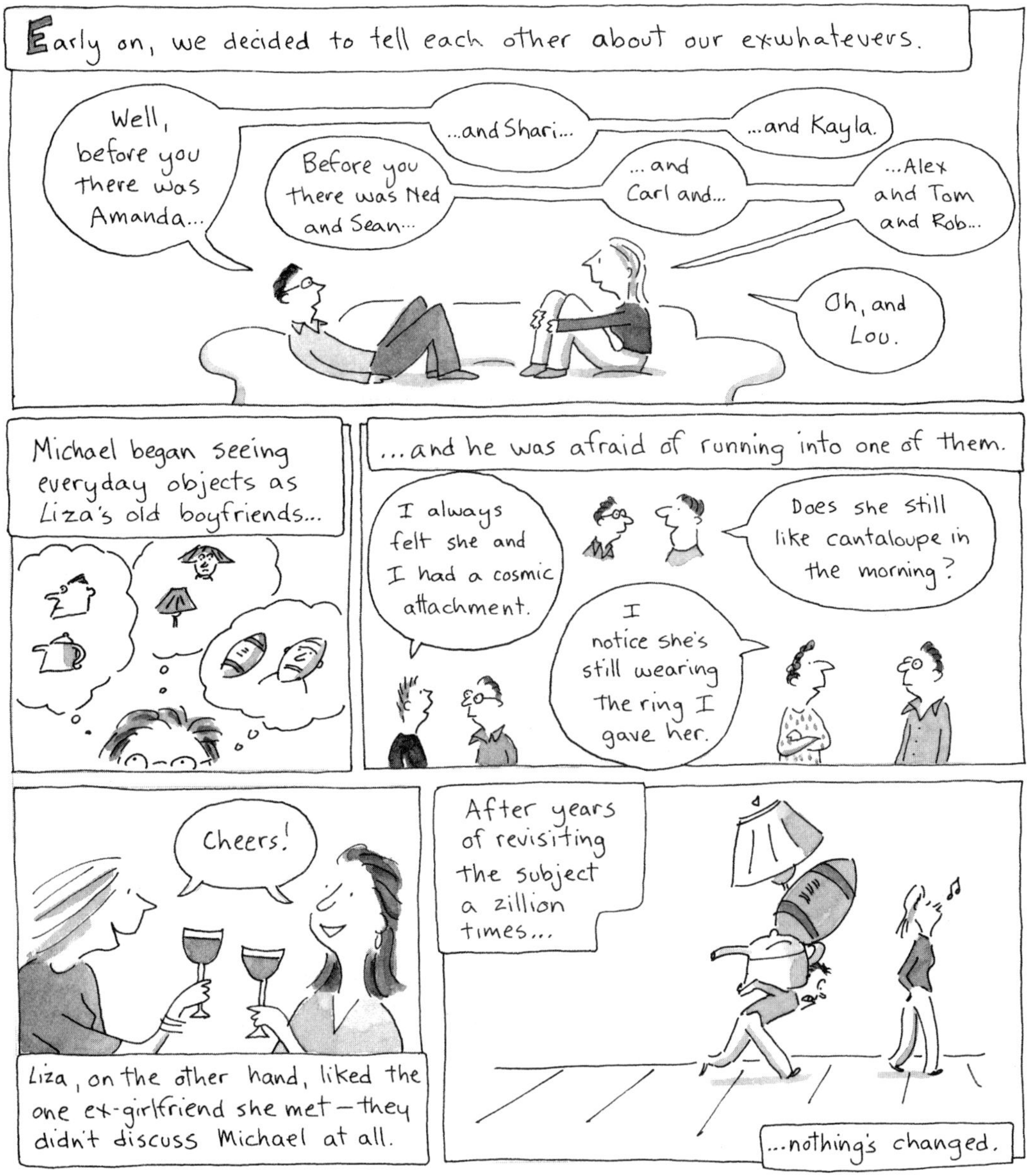
Early on, we decided to tell each other about our ex-whatevers.
Well, before you there was Amanda...
Before you there was Ned and Sean...
...and Shari...
...and Carl and...
...and Kayla.
...Alex and Tom and Rob...
Oh, and Lou.
Michael began seeing everyday objects as Liza's old boyfriends...
...and he was afraid of running into one of them.
I always felt she and I had a cosmic attachment.
Does she still like cantaloupe in the morning?
I notice she's still wearing the ring I gave her.
Cheers!
Liza, on the other hand, liked the one ex-girlfriend she met—they didn't discuss Michael at all.
After years of revisiting the subject a zillion times...
...nothing's changed.

"I love you, Zelda. I have always loved you—that is,
I have always loved you since I stopped always loving Mindy."

"My husband hates when I see old boyfriends,
but has said nothing about old girlfriends."

"At the first sign of trouble, he runs right back to his first wife."

"Hal was a better lover, but you have a better Vandyke."

"Ken, Avery—this is Rod. He refuses to be
lumped together with my old boyfriends."

"I was happily married once. It wasn't pretty."

"I'd be less than honest with you, Ned, if I said
I'd never shared a goblet of oysterettes
with anyone before."

"You said you'd blot me from your memory
forever and ever. _Now_ do you remember me?"

"My ex had a problem with me always asking him if he had a problem with me. Would _you_ have a problem with me always asking you if you had a problem with me?"

"Did Roger ever tell you about the time he and I
were locked in a marriage for two whole weeks?"

"Remember: No matter how many ex-husbands I have,
you'll always be the first."

"If you're the second wife of my first husband,
then I must be <u>your</u> first husband's third wife."

"My ex-husband's hide."

"What was he like when <u>you</u> were
in a shark cage with him?"

"Fifteen years ago. Santa Monica.
You were my bride—I was your groom. Remember?"

"I was involved with someone,
but that was a minute and a half ago."

"I bet you can't name all
my exes—in alphabetical order."

"Would it be all right if I still called every once in
a while, just to, y'know, scream at you?"

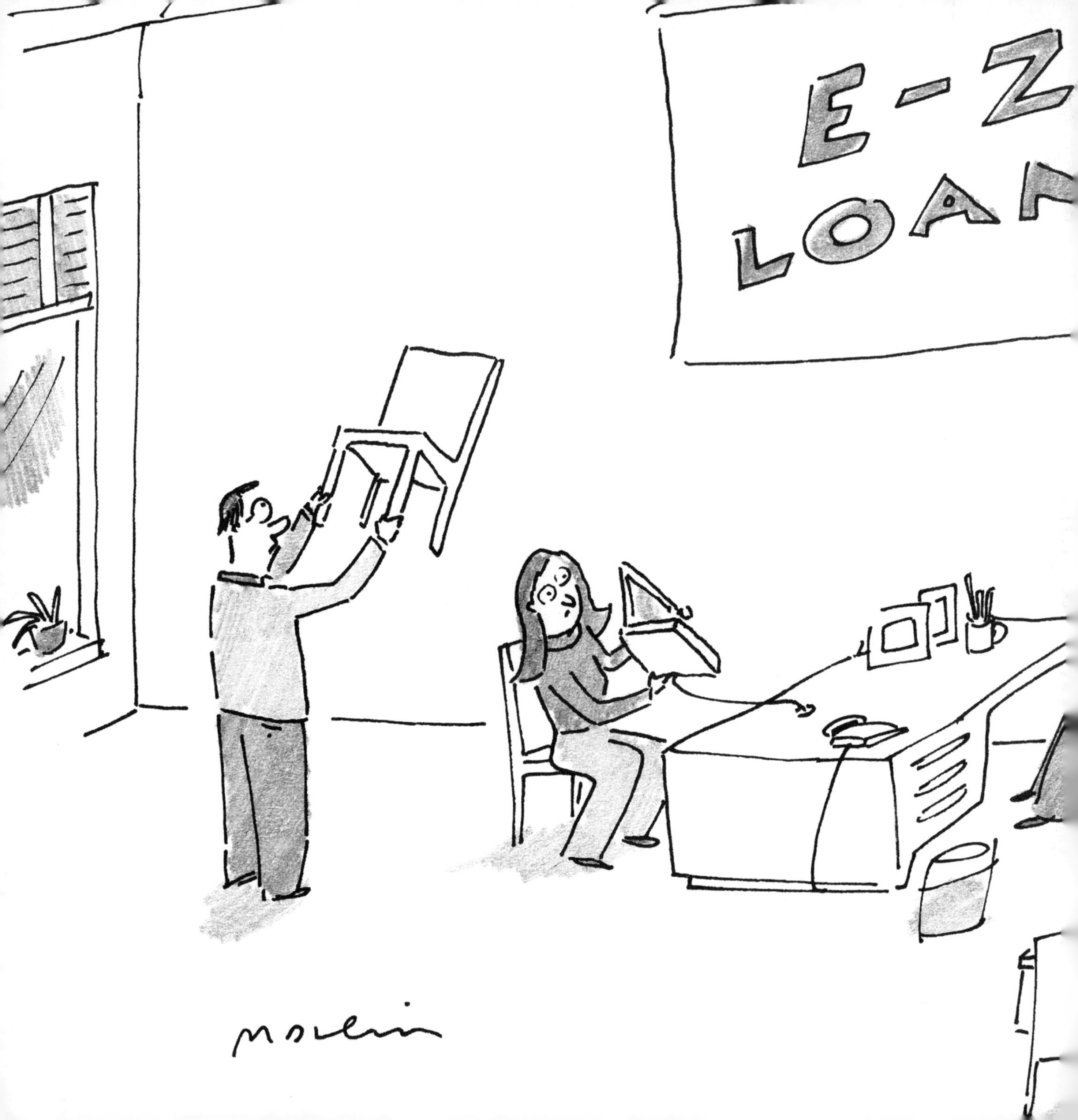
E-Z
LOAN

Is It Worth It?

It's Not <u>Your</u> Money.

Did you deposit that check?
  What check?
The one that came for you yesterday.
  Was it for that advertising job?
Which job was that?
  The one they wanted you to draw, but I did it.
Was that the one with gorillas in it?
  No, the one with hedgehogs.
Was it in color?
  Are you hungry?
Did you do sketches for it?
  I think so — too many for no money.
Wasn't there a lawyer involved?
  Yes, the one that died.
He died?!
  I'm having tuna. Want some?
  No, I'll just have ice cream.

But what about that check?

What check?

"I'm an optometrist, dear—optometrists don't 'kick ass.' "

"Of course the cat is paying our bills.
You don't think I'd let the dog do it?"

"John and Mary, having initialed these
last-minute changes to your prenup,
I pronounce you man and wife."

*"God bless Mom, God bless Dad, and
God bless our accountant."*

"Max, pull over—I smell a bargain."

"You see that dark, spooky image on the screen?
That's your credit history coming back to haunt you."

"I had to take out a loan to pay for this."

"Bond prices were up today, while most stocks,
and Edgar, remained unchanged."

"Look around all you want, Mr. and Mrs. Normley,
but I guarantee you won't find any hidden costs."

"You're so romantic, Gary, remembering
every intimate detail of our first audit together."

"O.K., we'll meet back here in about five hundred dollars."

"Him? He's our personal banker."

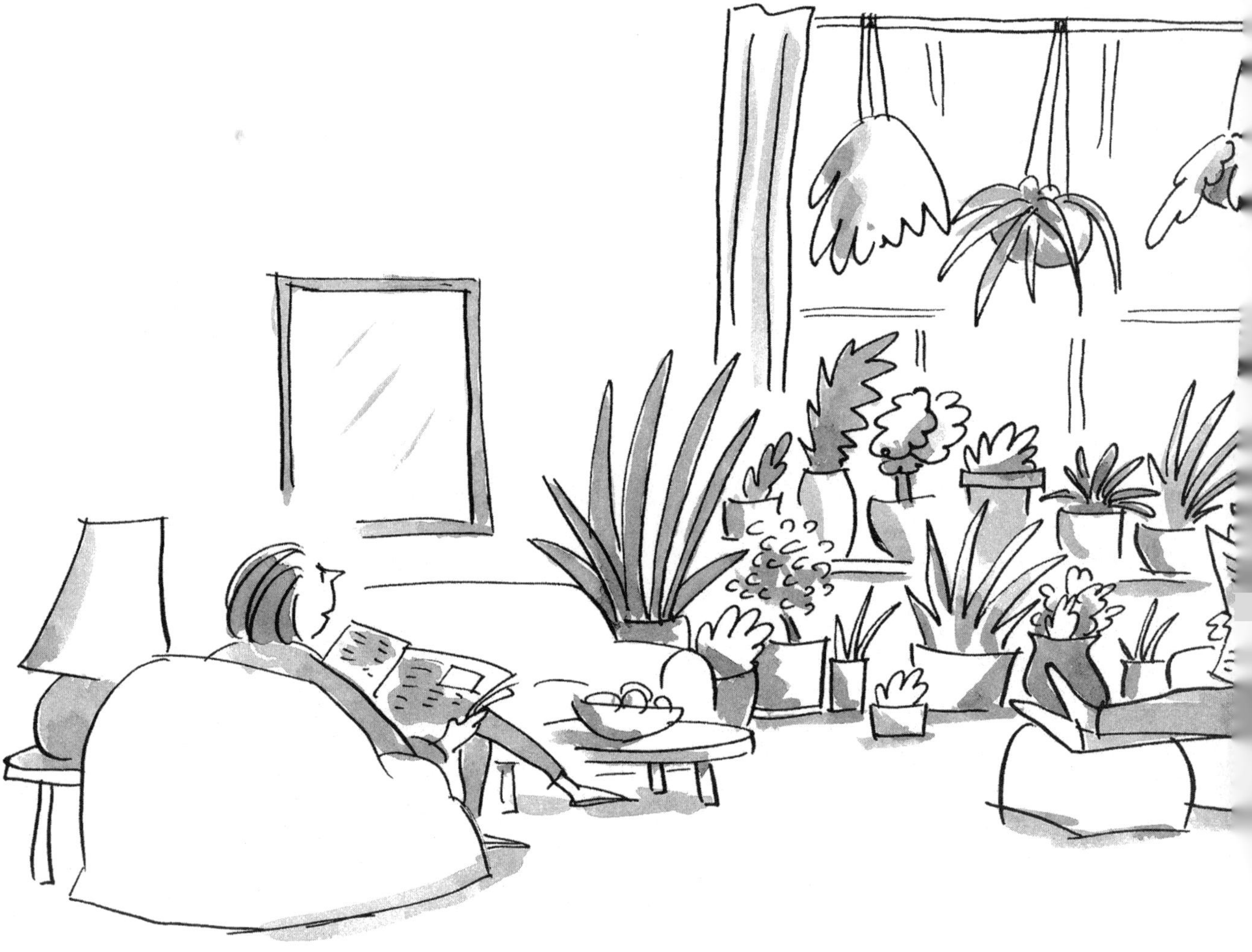

Obsessions and Possessions

I Can't Believe You Bought
Another One of Those.

DONNELLY

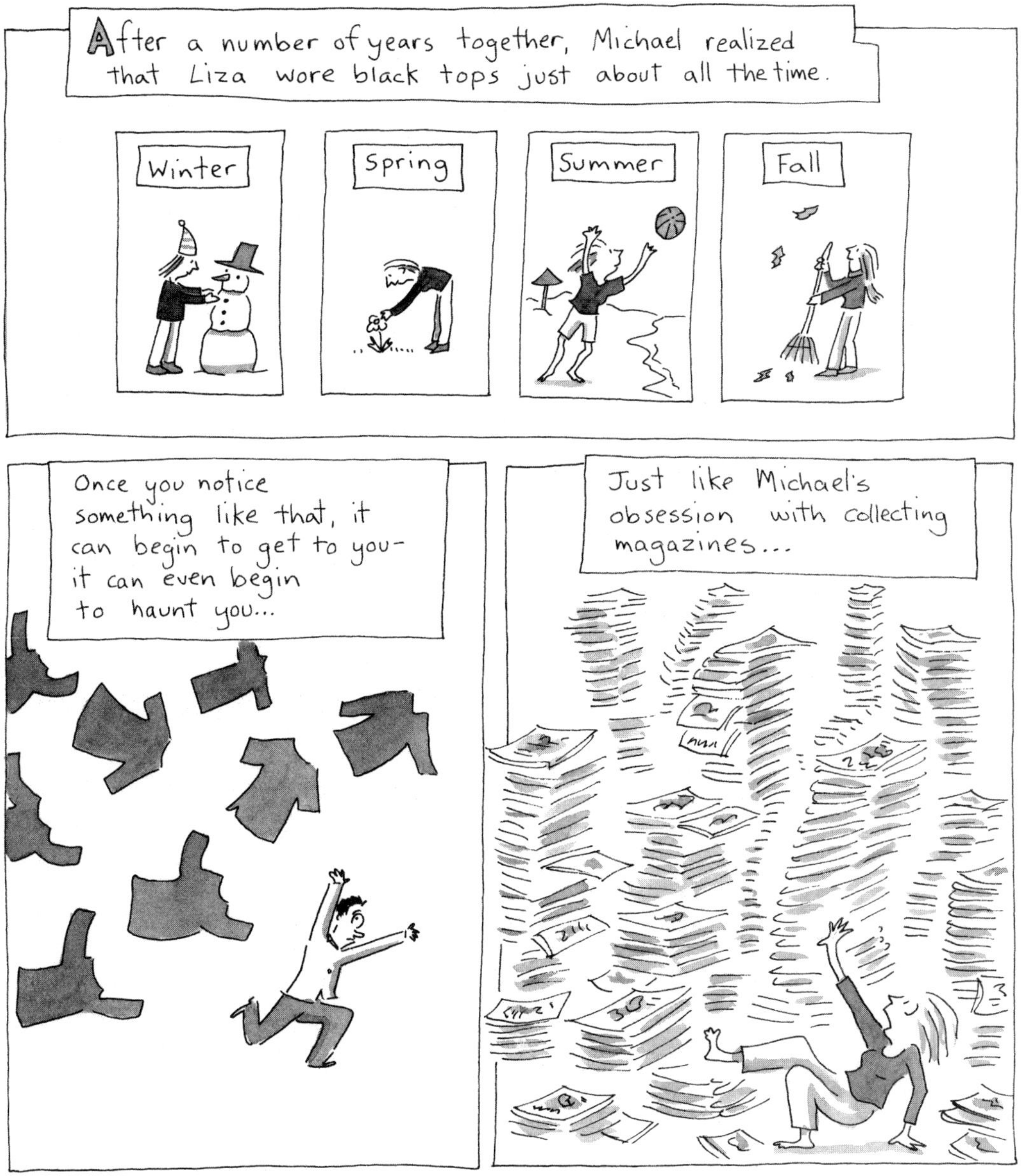
After a number of years together, Michael realized that Liza wore black tops just about all the time.
Winter
Spring
Summer
Fall
Once you notice something like that, it can begin to get to you- it can even begin to haunt you...
Just like Michael's obsession with collecting magazines...

"If she has one fault, it's that she can't
say 'no' to breadsticks."

"Well, if you didn't want cats,
why did you marry me?"

"I'll be in, honey, as soon as I rake the leaf."

"Thanks for the string, Mom. But you
should know: It's not for me, it's for Allen."

"Harold always puts the lights on the
tree and I always put the lights on Harold."

"Twenty-one years and twenty-one wind chimes ago,
she told me that she had bought her last wind chime.
And, like a fool, I believed her."

"I'd like you to consider changing your
morning routine of patting me and
kissing the dog goodbye."

"Have you been sneaking plants in again?"

"In the very unlikely event that
I stopped liking baseball, would you still love me?"

DONNELLY

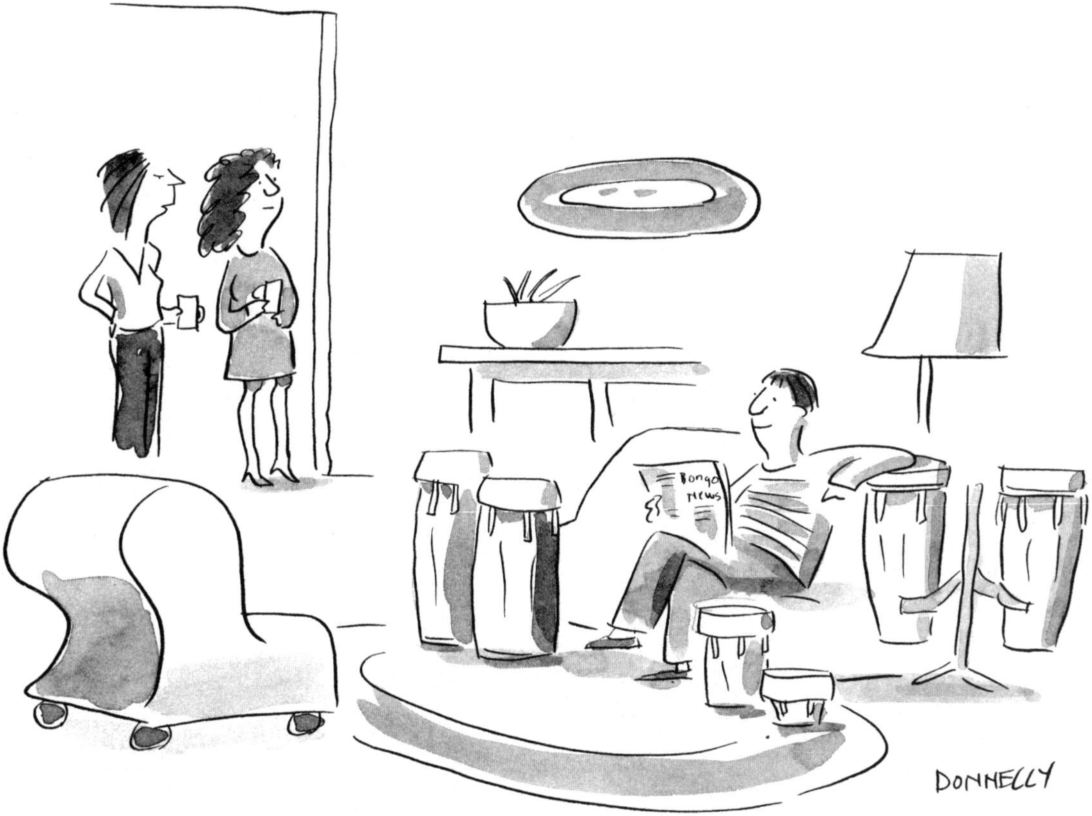
Bongo News
DONNELLY

"He came with bongos."

"Max has only one cup of coffee
a day, but it's a big cup."

"What's this five-hundred-and-twenty-seven-dollar
charge for free-range chickens?"

"For our anniversary, Marie gave me
a polo shirt with an alligator on it."

"If we break up, who gets the bicycle?"

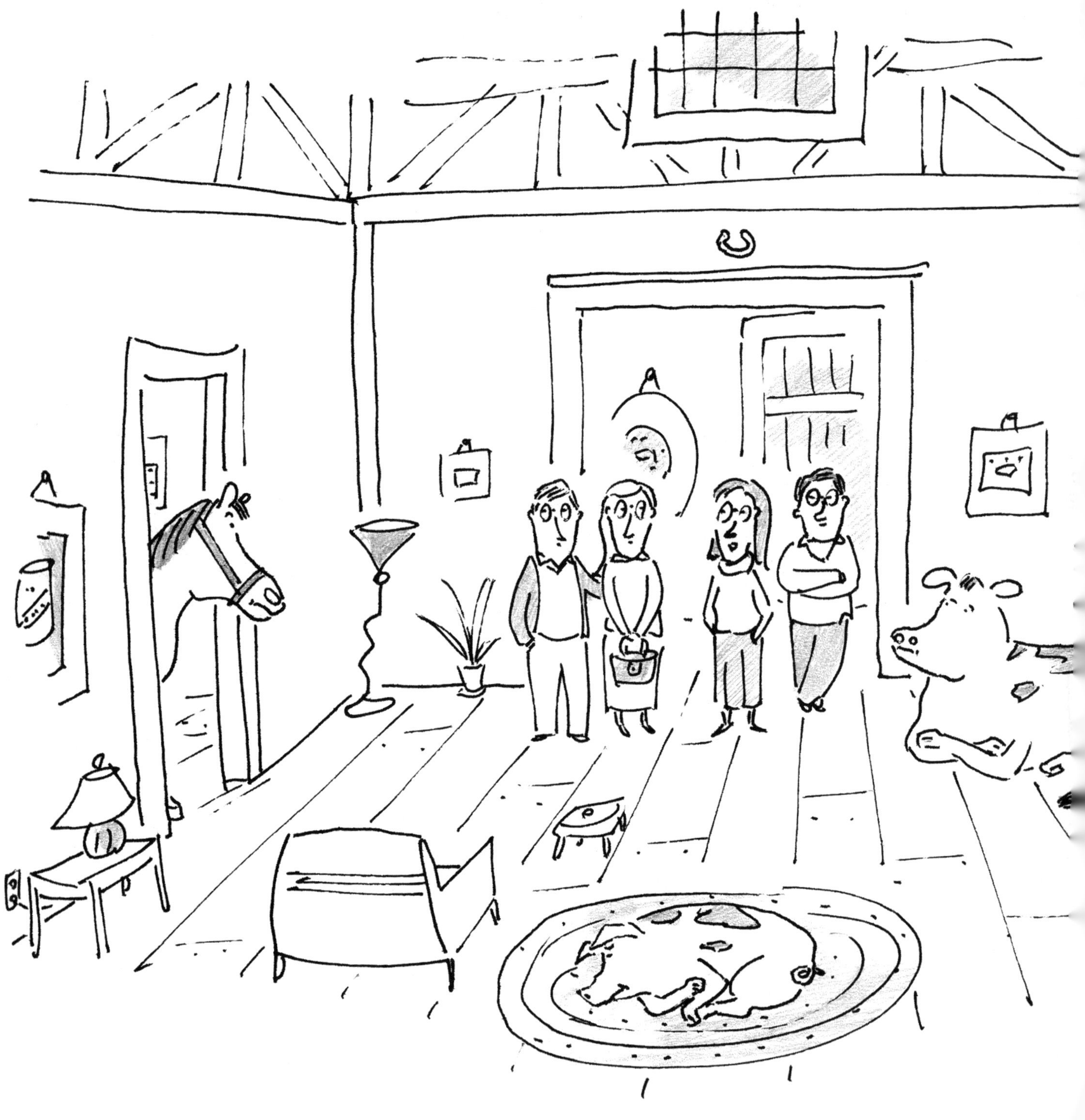

Friends Furry

What Is That Smell?

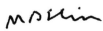

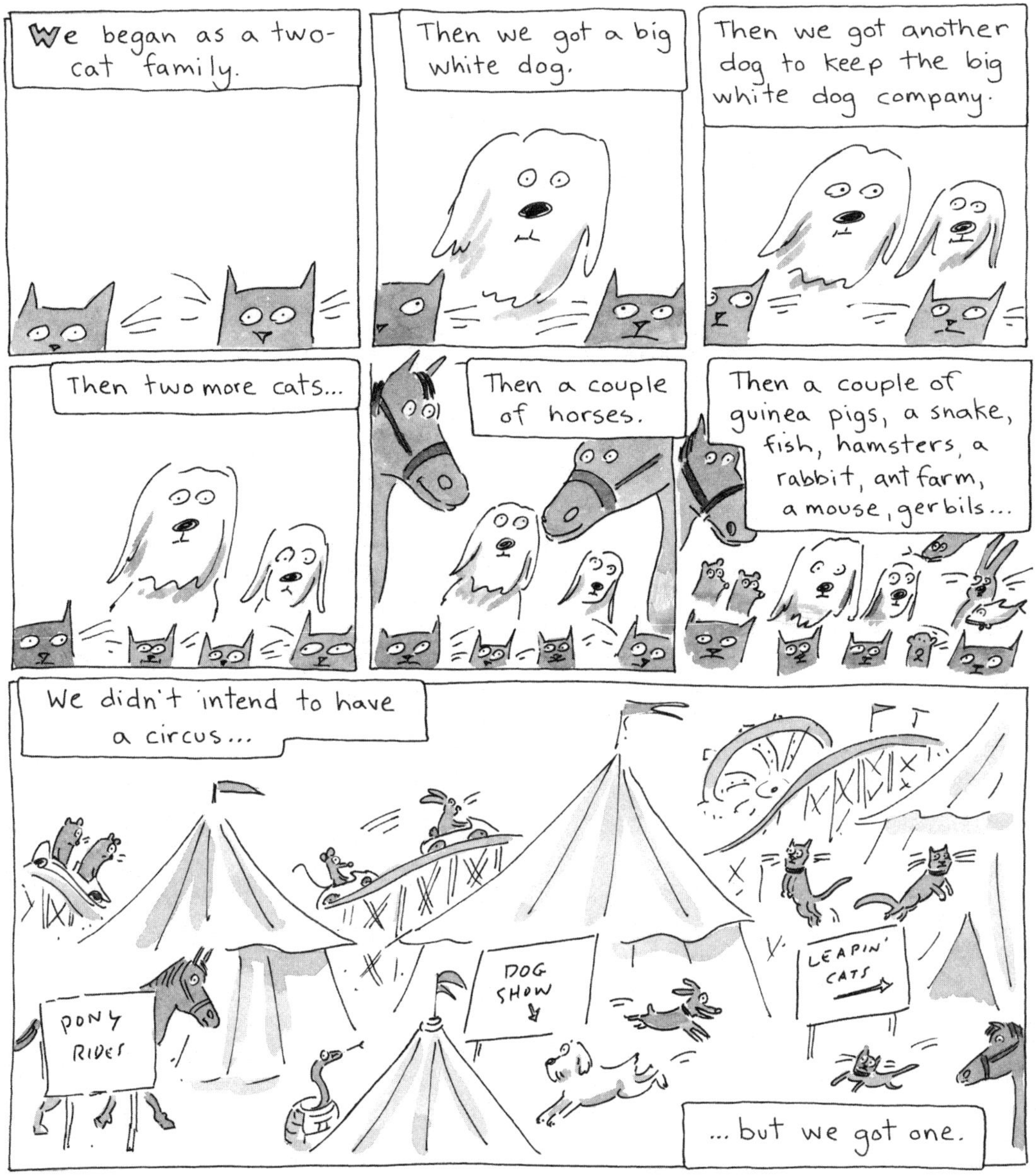
We began as a two-cat family.
Then we got a big white dog.
Then we got another dog to keep the big white dog company.
Then two more cats...
Then a couple of horses.
Then a couple of guinea pigs, a snake, fish, hamsters, a rabbit, ant farm, a mouse, gerbils...
We didn't intend to have a circus...
PONY RIDES
DOG SHOW
LEAPIN' CATS
...but we got one.

"*My pets—Mark's pets.*"

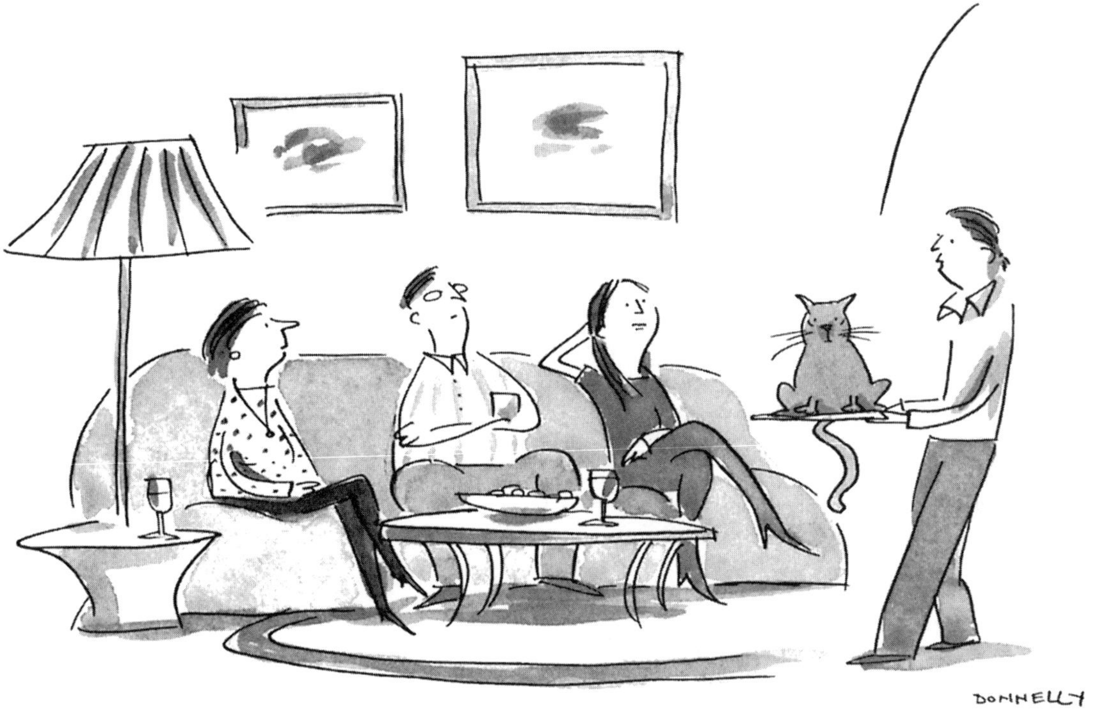
DONNELLY

"Cat, anyone?"

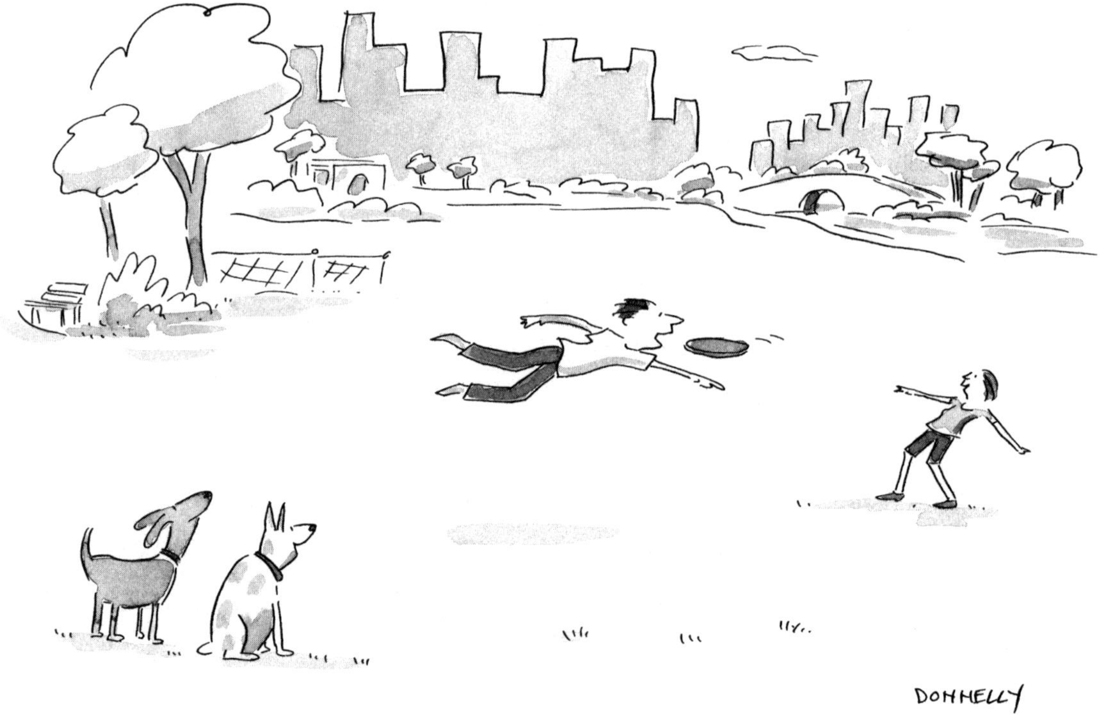
DONNELLY

"I taught him that!"

"You want a child, I want a dog. Can't we compromise?"

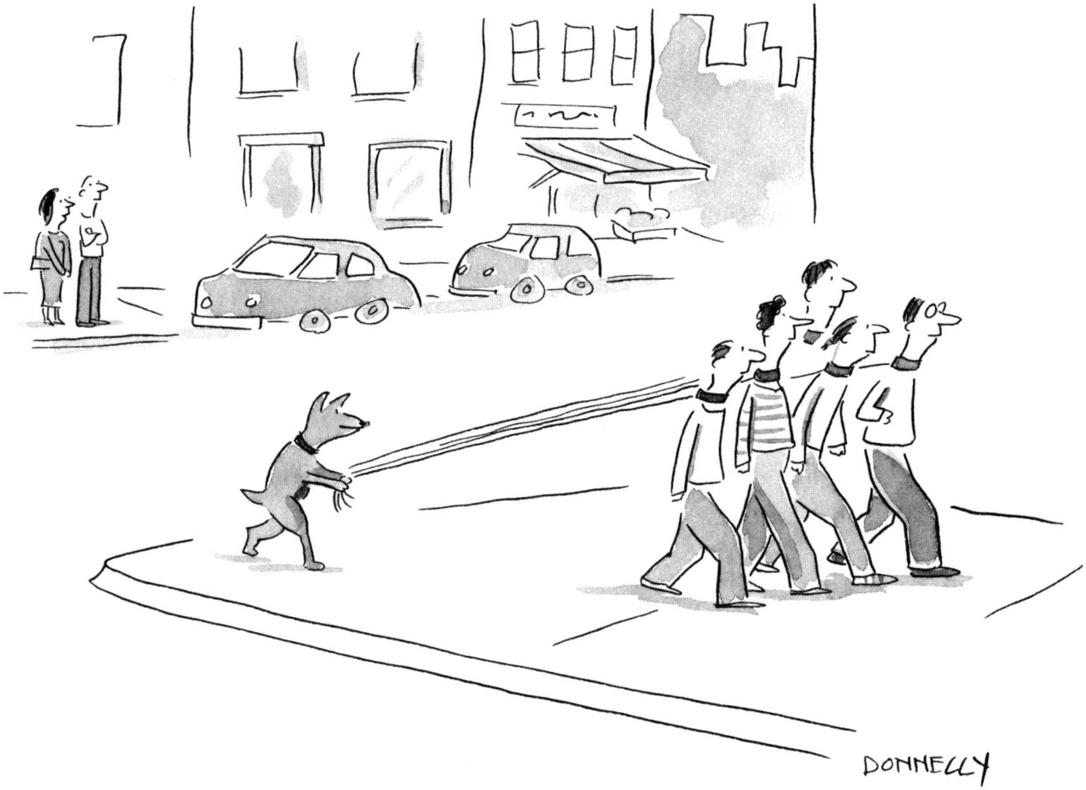
DONNELLY

"Husband walker."

"As this was originally a barn,
we've tried to maintain some of the flavor."

"Where's your mousse? I can't find mine."

"I've lost track: Whose turn is it to
scratch the cat?"

"He brings these things home
and I end up taking care of them."

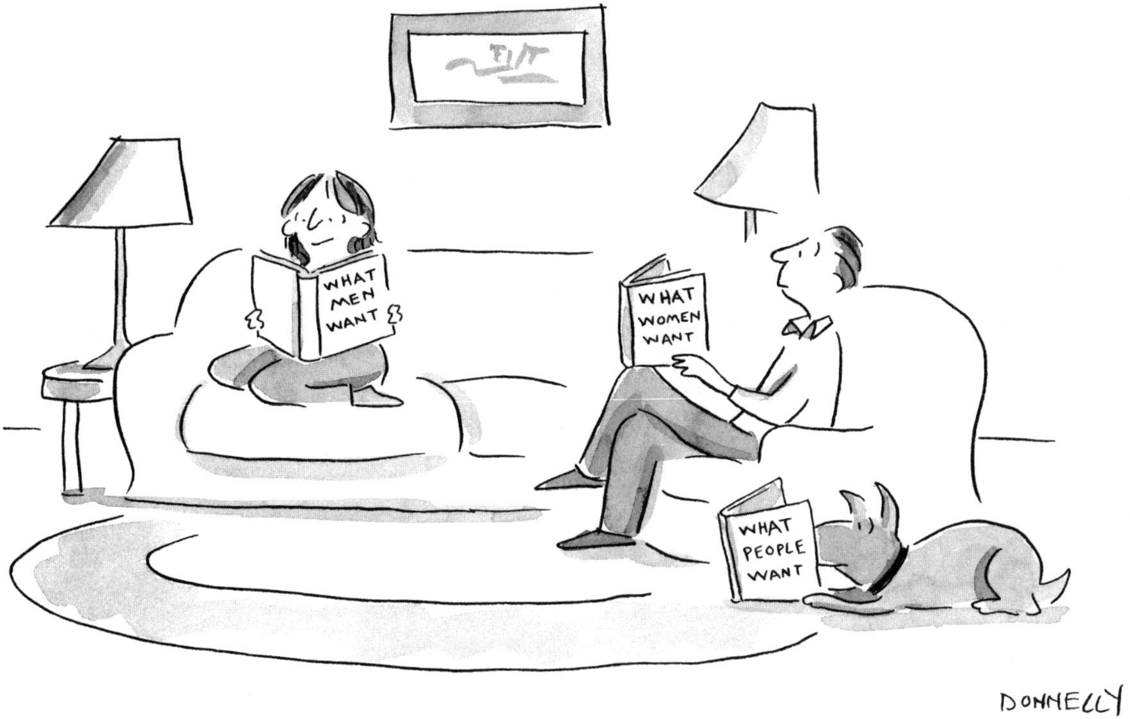
WHAT MEN WANT
WHAT WOMEN WANT
WHAT PEOPLE WANT
DONNELLY

"All right, I was wrong. A Shih Tzu was _not_ all that
was missing from our marriage."

"*My God, you're right! Kenny is a hedgehog!*"

"It would be nice if at least one of you
wagged your tail when I came home."

"So which one had the fur ball?"

"Honey, I asked you not to use the cat that way."

"You'd think that if we remembered getting the cat and dog,
we'd remember getting the potbellied pig."

"This was a good idea—they really needed to get out."

"You see—Spot wasn't a rock-climbing dog until
Kiki became a rock-climbing cat."

"It's true—Ken had more money,
but you have more dogs."

"Not tonight. The cat is in my lap."

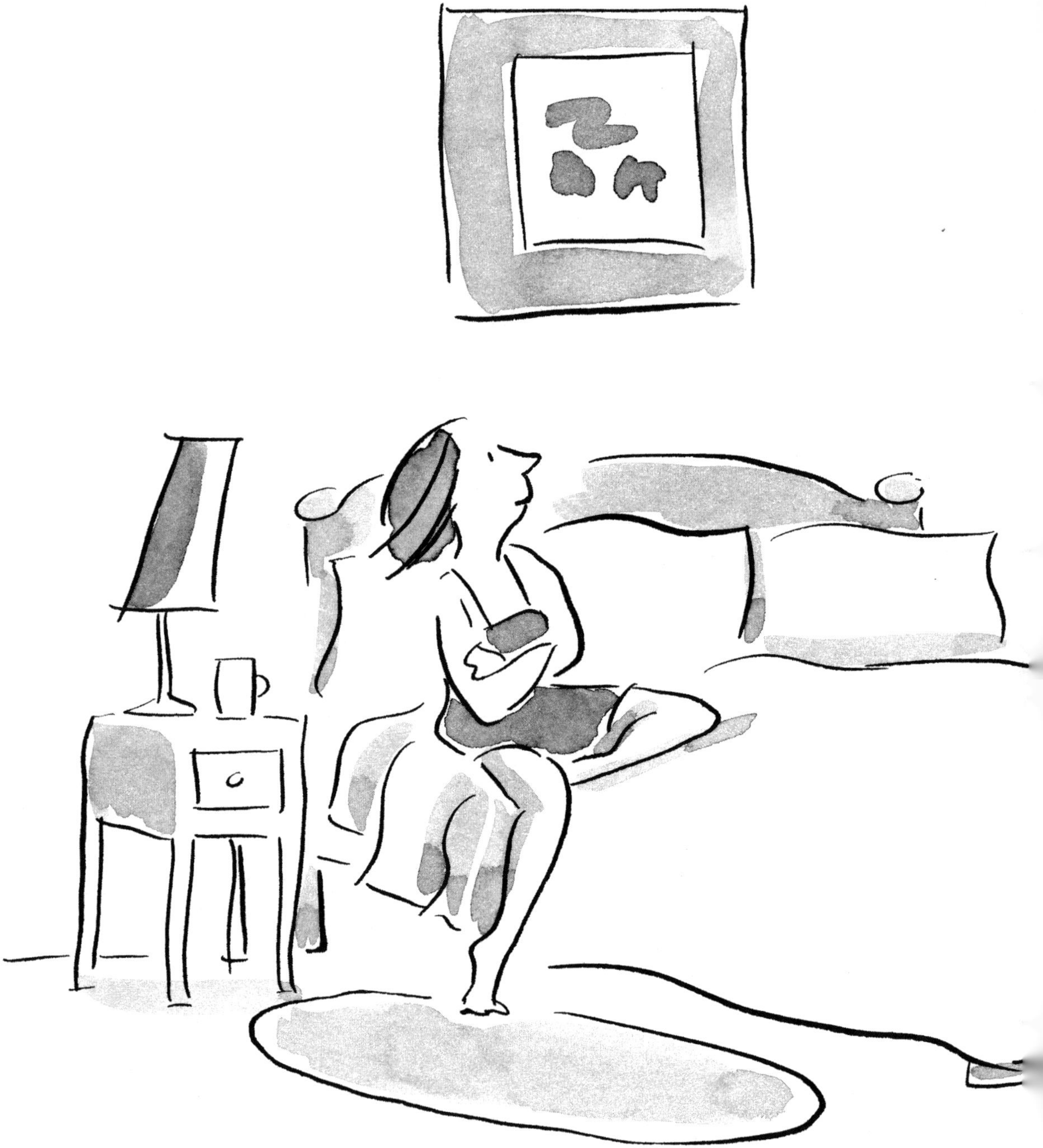

Come Hither

Remind Me, What Does
That Look Mean Again?

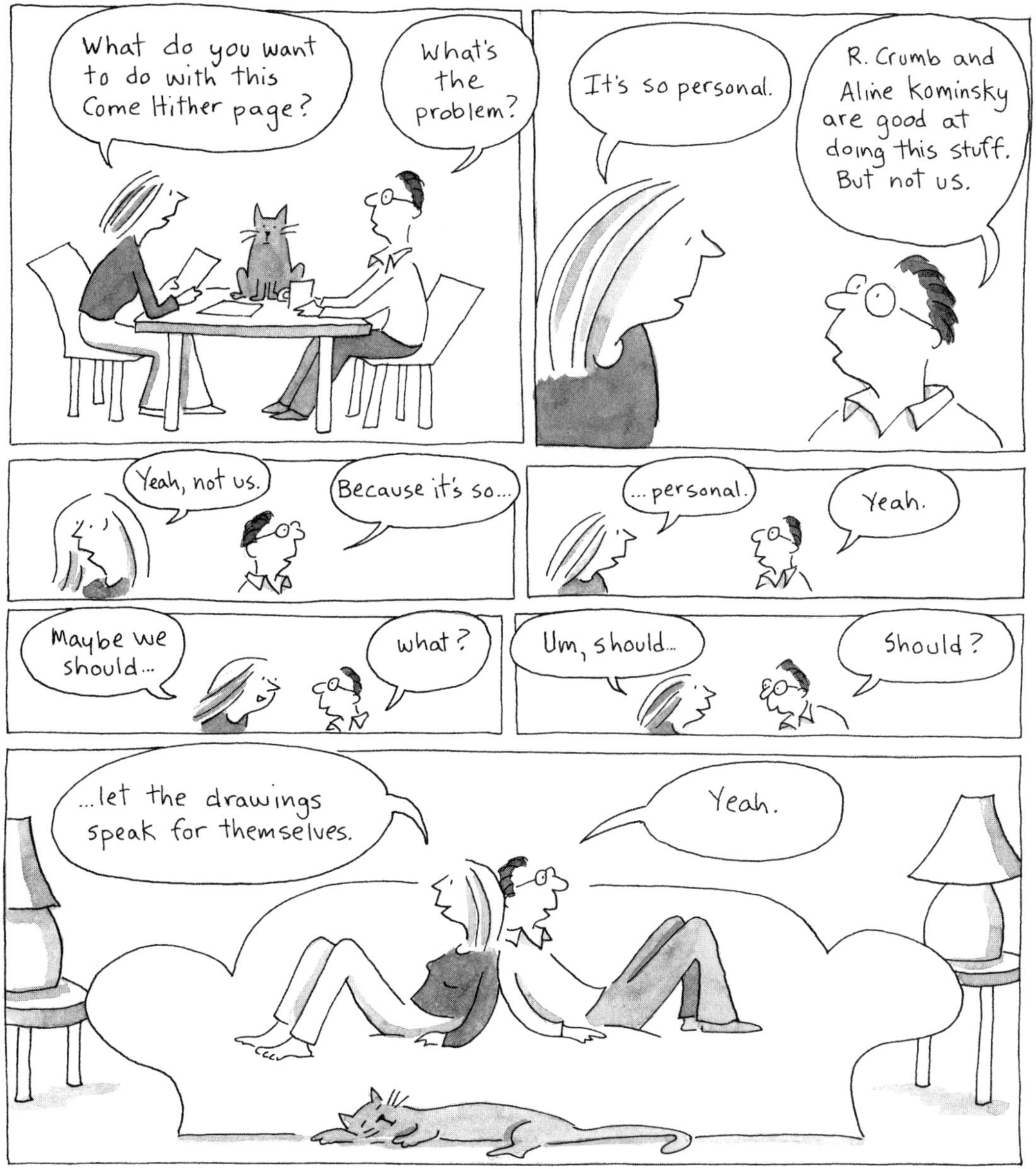
What do you want to do with this Come Hither page?
What's the problem?
It's so personal.
R. Crumb and Aline Kominsky are good at doing this stuff. But not us.
Yeah, not us.
Because it's so...
...personal.
Yeah.
Maybe we should...
what?
Um, should...
Should?
...let the drawings speak for themselves.
Yeah.

"I couldn't remember if you said you
wanted to clown around or fool around tonight."

"We're married, Harold, not fused."

"A little moonlight and a lot of chlorinated water
makes me say the craziest things."

"No, it wasn't his looks that first attracted me.
It was the sound of his flip-flops."

"That's not my heart beating—my cell phone's vibrating."

"Is tonight the night we, statistically,
are to have sex?"

"*Well, are you going to invade my space or not?*"

"Hey look, before this goes any further,
I should probably tell you we're married."

"I guess you didn't get my text."

"We should look upside down
at each other more often."

"You want me to shift my strategy?"

"Gary, we need to not talk."

"I know you're trying to tell me something with the scooter,
but I can't tell what."

"Perhaps you misunderstood: I was suggesting
we get emotionally naked."

"Would you like a little sex with your coffee?"

"I'll be right back—I'm going to blink."

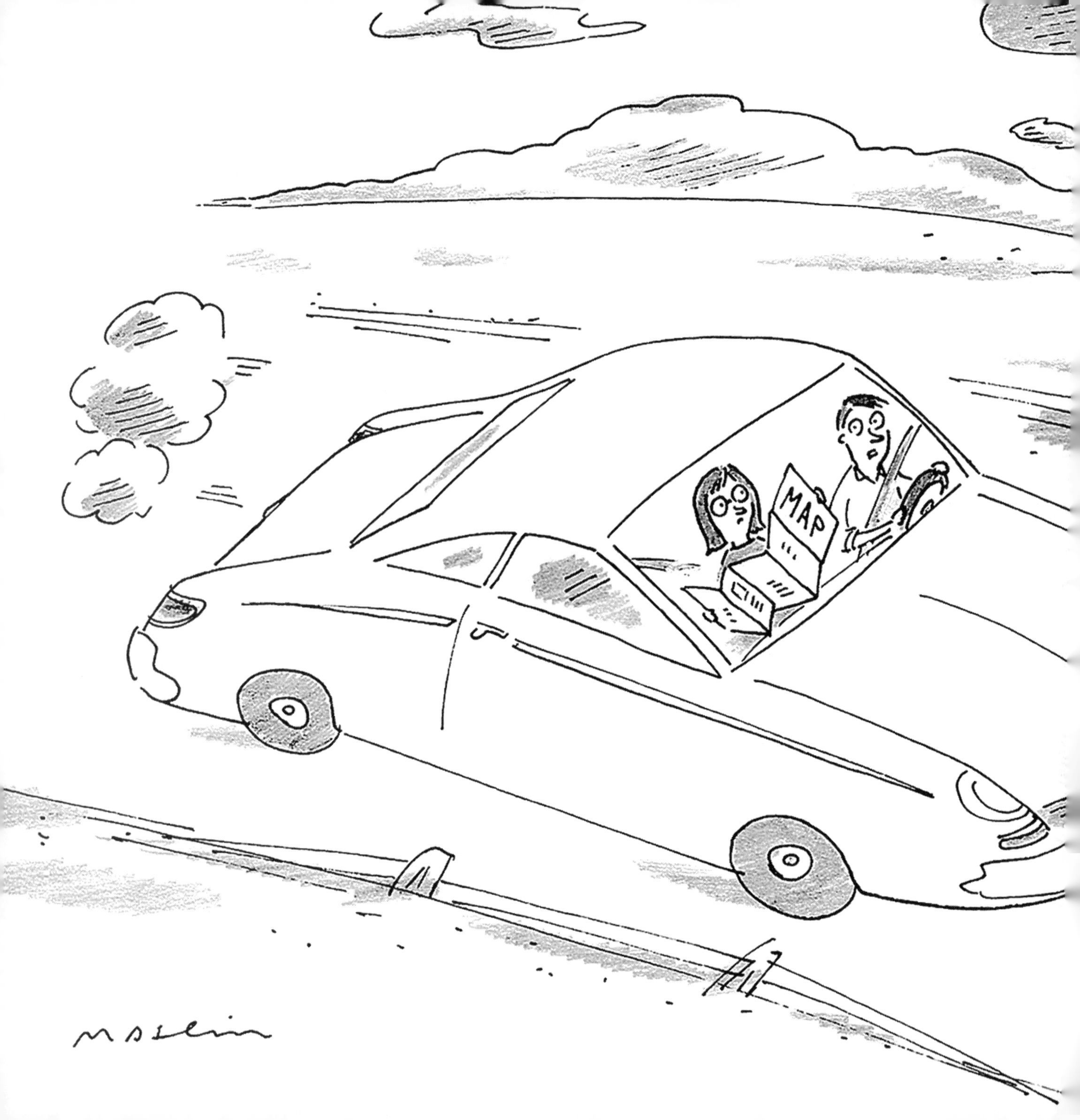
MAP

In the Ring

*Why Can't We All Just
Get Along?*

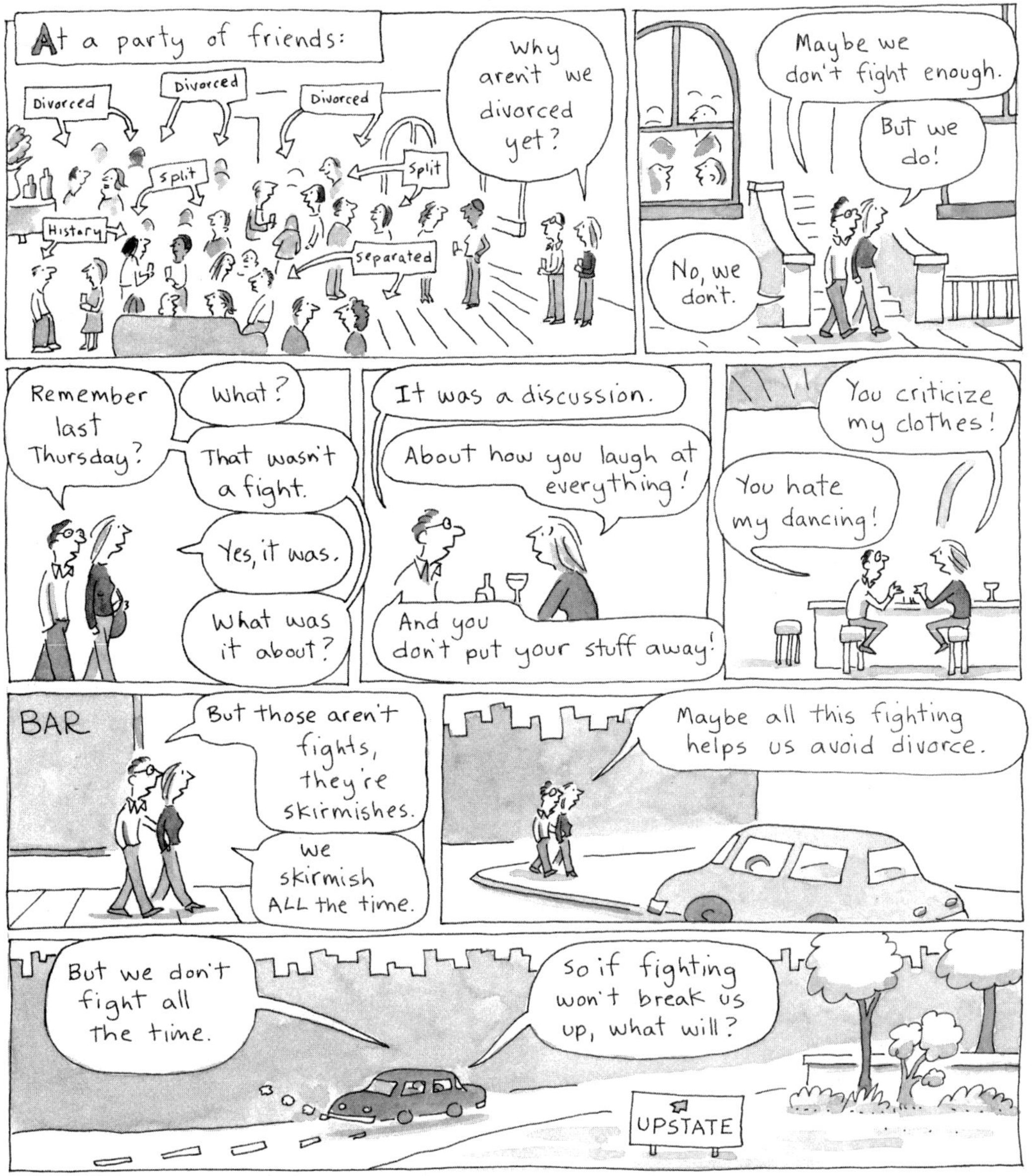
At a party of friends:
Divorced
Divorced
Divorced
Split
Split
History
Separated
Why aren't we divorced yet?
Maybe we don't fight enough.
But we do!
No, we don't.
Remember last Thursday?
What?
That wasn't a fight.
Yes, it was.
What was it about?
It was a discussion.
About how you laugh at everything!
And you don't put your stuff away!
You criticize my clothes!
You hate my dancing!
BAR
But those aren't fights, they're skirmishes.
we skirmish ALL the time.
Maybe all this fighting helps us avoid divorce.
But we don't fight all the time.
So if fighting won't break us up, what will?
UPSTATE

"Cool! My new cell phone allows me to see your angry face
as well as hear your angry voice."

"Since we're both working on the same marriage, I thought
it would be a good idea to get together and compare notes."

"Oh yeah? Well, I'm not remembering
you in _my_ memoirs!"

"Before this marriage goes any further,
let's get something straight: I'm _darling_ and you're _dear_."

Newlyweds

Three years of marriage

Ten years of marriage

Twenty-five years of marriage

"My wife says when I wear it,
it reminds her too much of me."

"It would take more than your pleats to drive us apart, but not much more."

"That's right, Artie: just float there
and pretend you don't hear me."

"You throw the chair, I delete your files."

"And now I'd like to do my impersonation of a happily married woman."

"*I'm* impenetrable?"

"Any other pains besides
your husband?"

"O.K., step away from the laptop and hold up
your end of the conversation."

"How many miles before our next fight?"

"You could at least acknowledge the fact
that I'm ignoring you."

"Do you want _me_ to tell you what's on your mind
or do you want _you_ to tell me what's on your mind?"

"That you never ever annoy me is
beginning to annoy me."

"Oh right, of course you didn't hear me.
That was my inner voice telling you to shut up."

"It's not a possibility now, but when the kids are grown
Sam and I figure we'll have time for a divorce."

"Is there *nothing* I can say or do
to help destroy this marriage?"

"You know what I'd love? I'd love it if you'd do that thing you do when you storm out of the house and disappear for weeks, and sometimes months on end."

"I think we should stop fooling ourselves
and begin fooling other people."

"I've got him right where I want him, now that I don't want him."

"Let's face it, Tony—there's only
one thing keeping this marriage together."

"We've put so much effort into breaking up it would be a shame not to."

"I hear their marriage is in trouble."

"*I'm giving __you__ up for New Year's.*"

"What, no goodbye finger?"

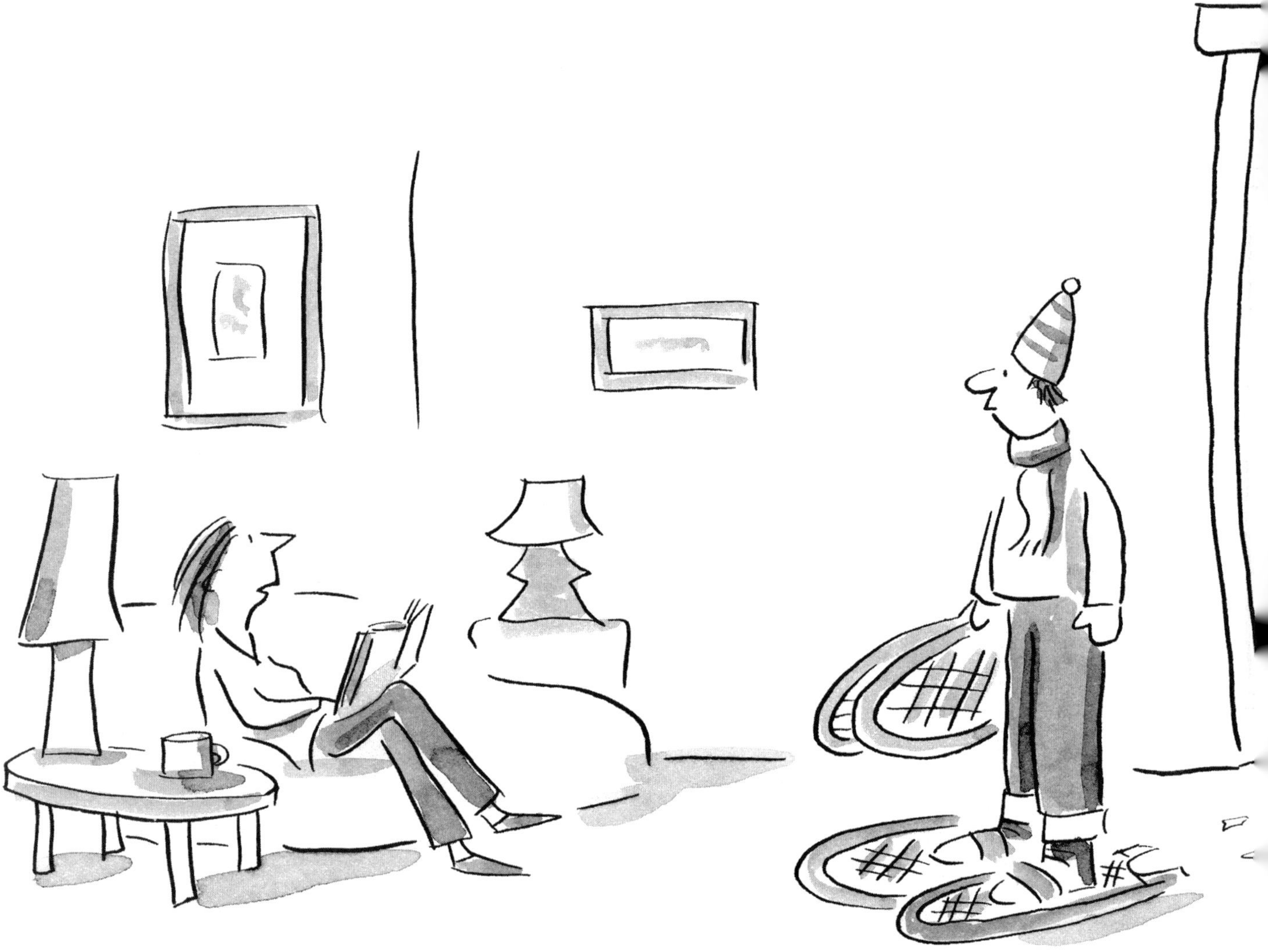

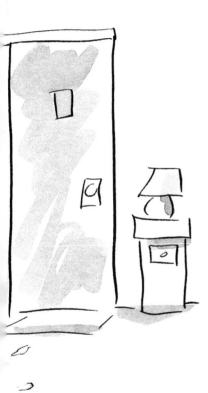

Play with Me

You Call That Fun?

DONNELLY

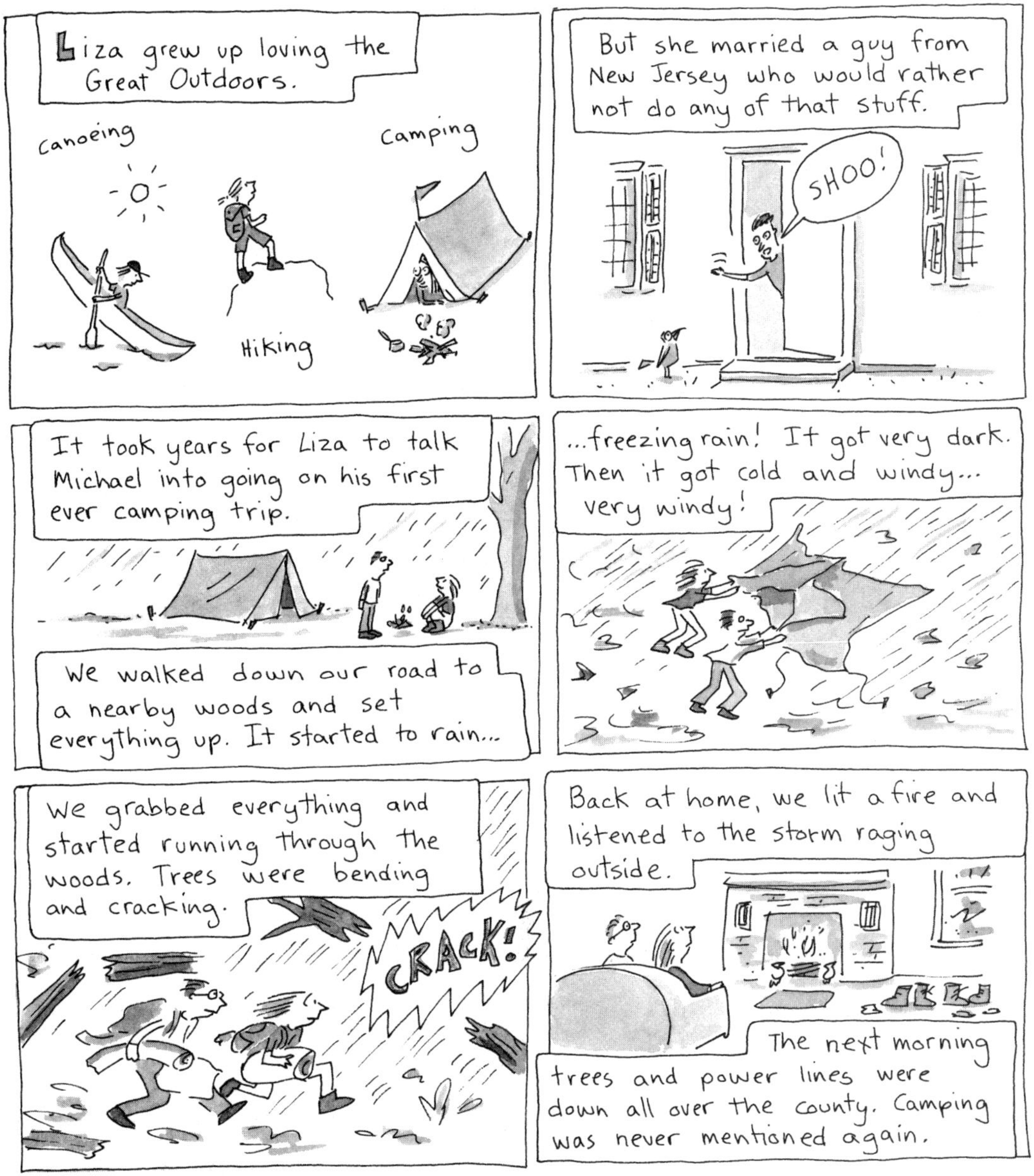
Liza grew up loving the Great Outdoors.
Canoeing
Hiking
Camping
But she married a guy from New Jersey who would rather not do any of that stuff.
SHOO!
It took years for Liza to talk Michael into going on his first ever camping trip.
We walked down our road to a nearby woods and set everything up. It started to rain...
...freezing rain! It got very dark. Then it got cold and windy... very windy!
We grabbed everything and started running through the woods. Trees were bending and cracking.
CRACK!
Back at home, we lit a fire and listened to the storm raging outside.
The next morning trees and power lines were down all over the county. Camping was never mentioned again.

"It does come as somewhat of a surprise, Carla.
I thought marriage was a roller-coaster ride."

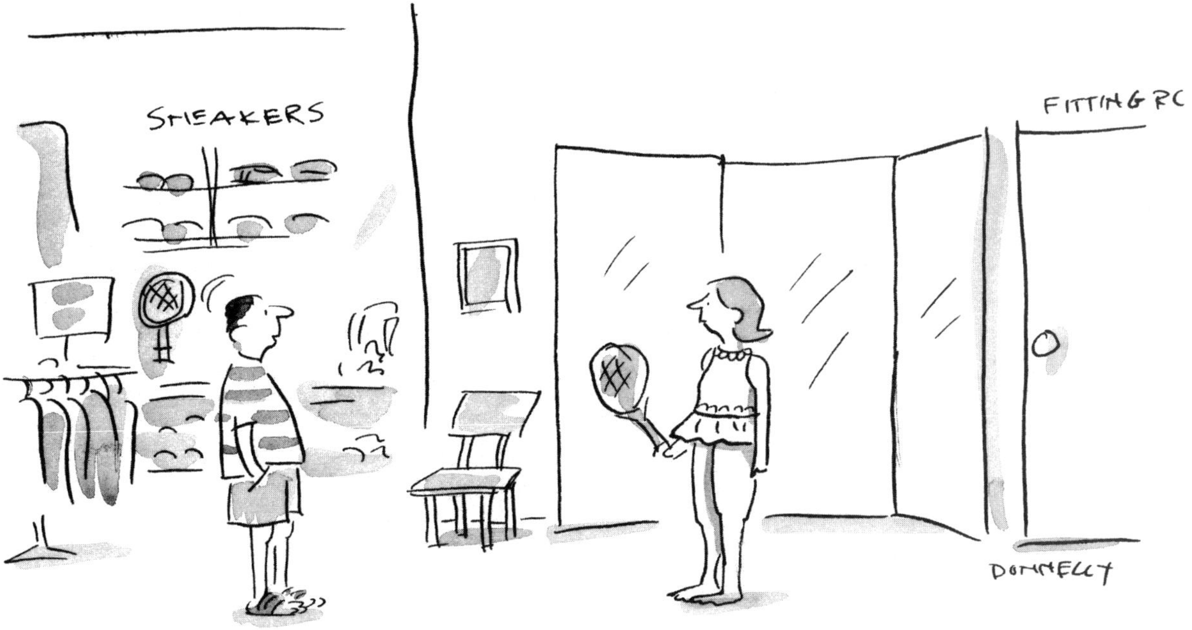
SNEAKERS
FITTING RC
DONNELLY

"Now rush the net."

"What I wanted you to do was pick me up and carry me, kicking and screaming, down to the water, and throw me into the waves. That's what I _wanted_ you to do. I don't want you to do that anymore."

THE EGGLEYS
WORKING HARD,
PLAYING HARD
FOR TWENTY-
FOUR YEARS

"You don't have to go to this party. It's 'Men Optional.'"

"Our vows said 'in sickness and in health.'
There was nothing about 'in snowshoeing.' "

"Could you lend me a hand dragging my husband
out of shallow water and into the open sea?"

"You can't bluff in a twenty-year-old marriage, dear."

"If we're going to run with the bulls at Pamplona,
we're going to need better shoes."

"We're sharing midlife crises."

"When, exactly, did it occur to you that the thing lacking
in our marriage was a little Silly Putty?"

"Remember the good old days when
we faced in the same direction?"

"Push me really high, just like you did when we were first married."

"Is that an inflatable sea horse, or are you just glad to see me?"

"Glide or get off the glider."

"You'll never move on until you learn to let go."

"*I bet you'd walk the beach with me if
we weren't wearing our matching bathing suits.*"

"If we're not going bowling,
I'd rather you didn't wear your bowling shirt."

"He'd make a good husband.
He doesn't dance."

"Now it looks like a face, now it looks like a shoe,
now it looks like a beagle, now it looks like a footstool . . ."

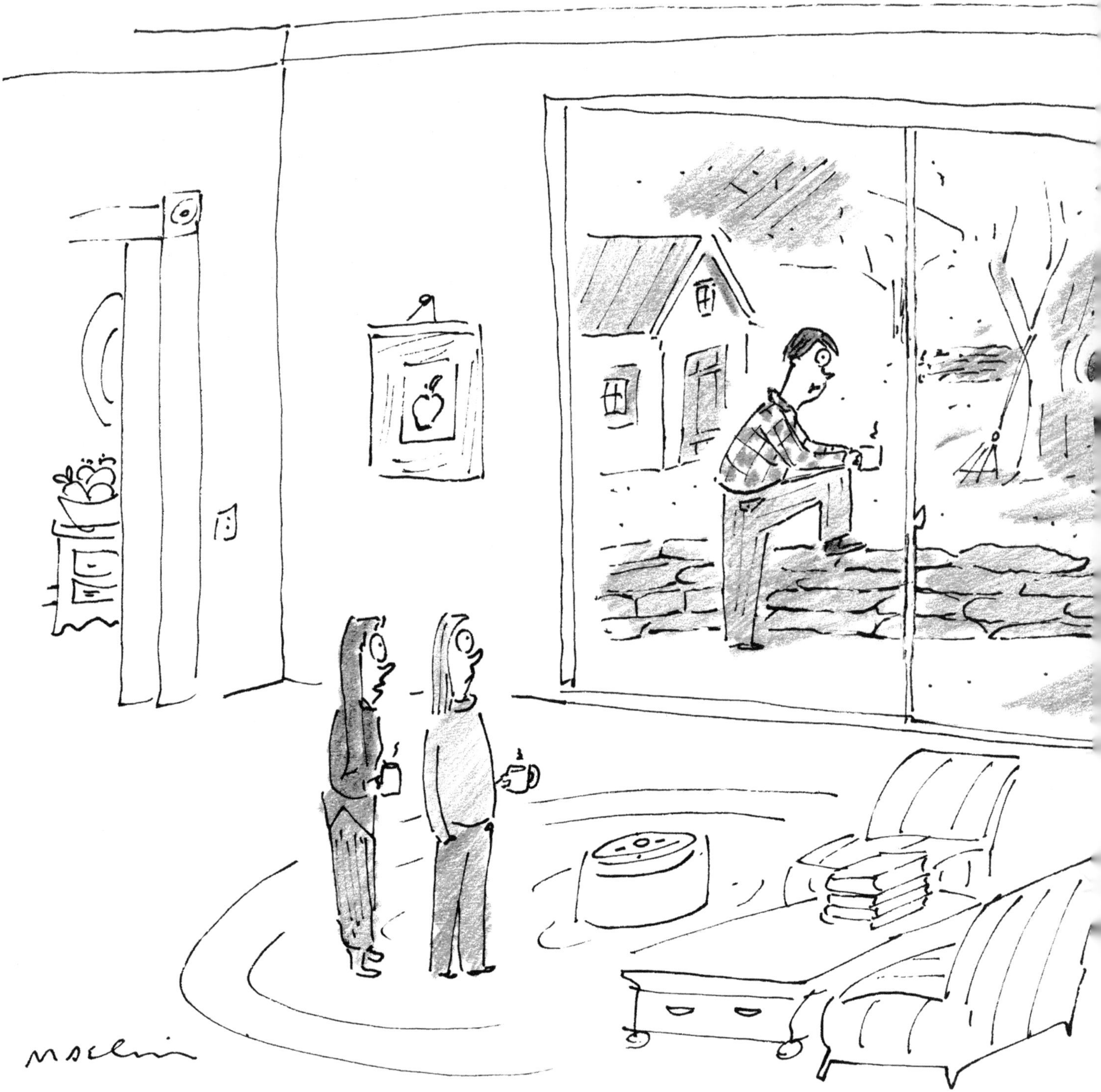

Hearth Happenings

This Is Living.

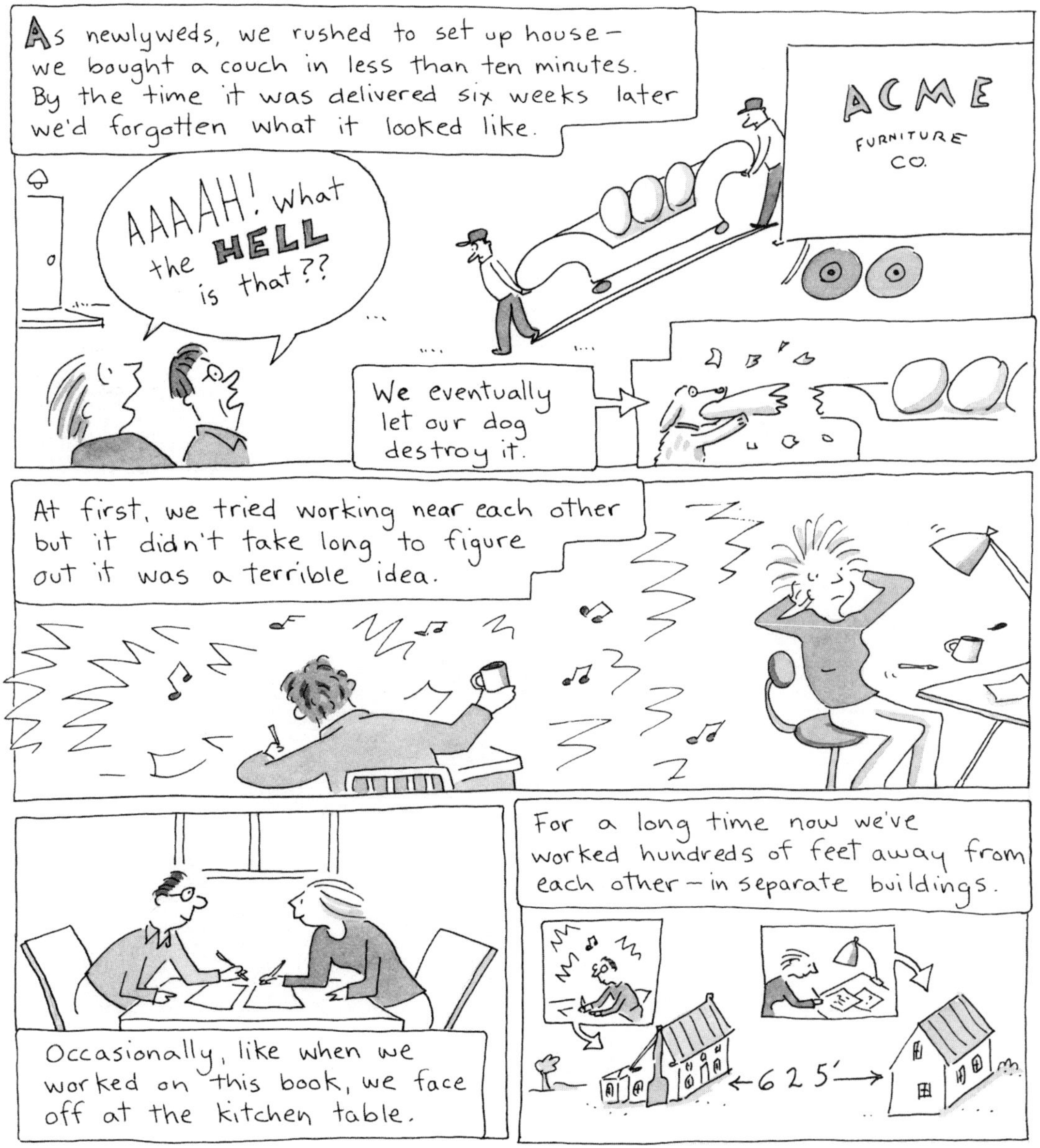
As newlyweds, we rushed to set up house—we bought a couch in less than ten minutes. By the time it was delivered six weeks later we'd forgotten what it looked like.
ACME FURNITURE CO.
AAAAH! What the HELL is that??
...
...
...
We eventually let our dog destroy it.
At first, we tried working near each other but it didn't take long to figure out it was a terrible idea.
Occasionally, like when we worked on this book, we face off at the kitchen table.
For a long time now we've worked hundreds of feet away from each other—in separate buildings.
625'

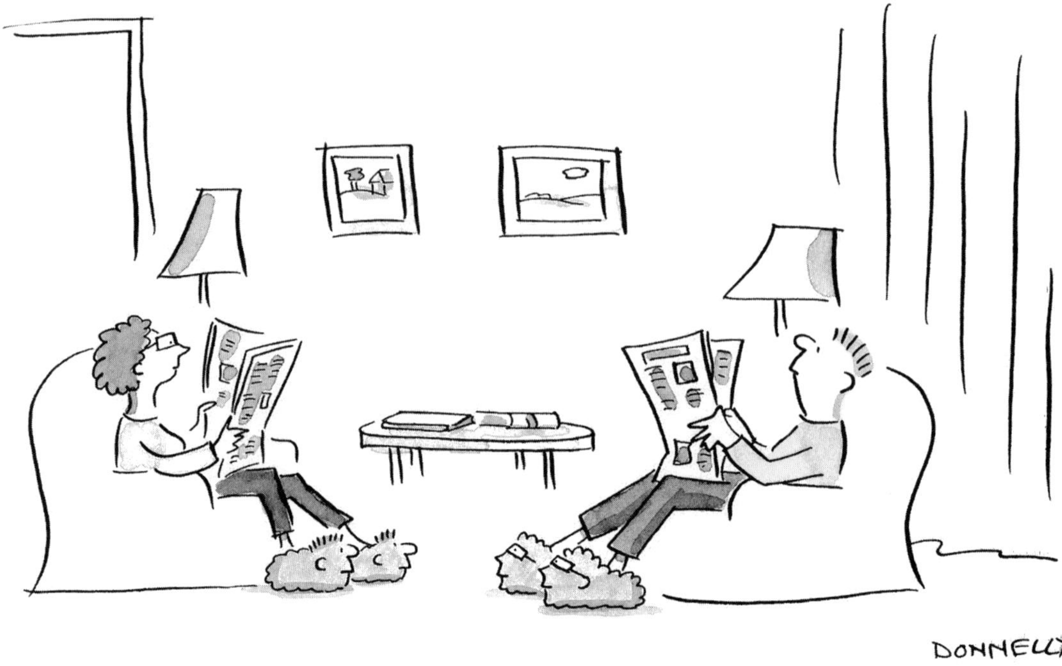
DONNELLY

"The slipcovers are darling, and I just _love_
what you've done with your husband."

"I brought out the grill and Henry, but I haven't uncovered them yet."

"No, he hasn't lost any weight—he's just wearing humongous pants."

"Some of it was done with wood, screws,
and nails—but most of it's done with mirrors."

"See you in the fall, sweetie."

"I really should go—Kyle's still stuck in his turtleneck."

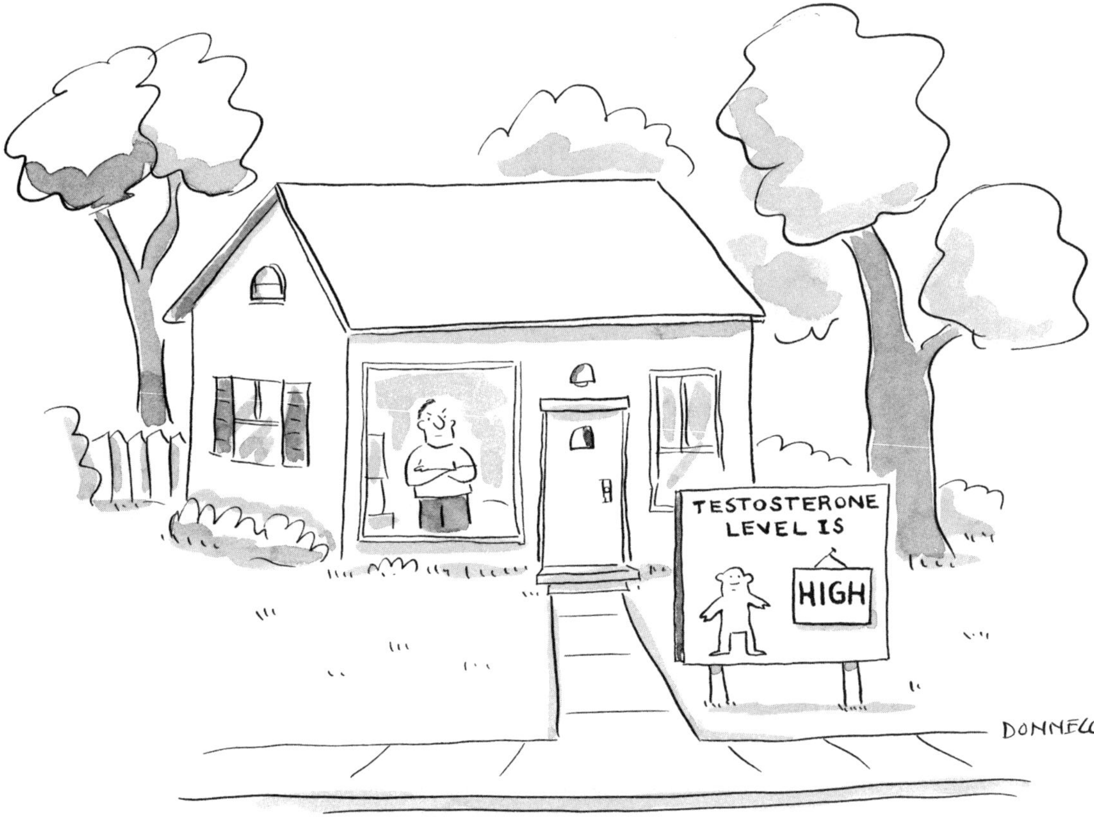
TESTOSTERONE
LEVEL IS
HIGH
DONNELLY

"And this is where I go to escape
from where I go to escape."

"Can you _please_ dust the coconuts—
we have company coming!"

"Shall we wash them or
throw them at each other?"

"Nothing but French Provincial all these years,
then—whammo! The Country Look."

"That's his favorite section."

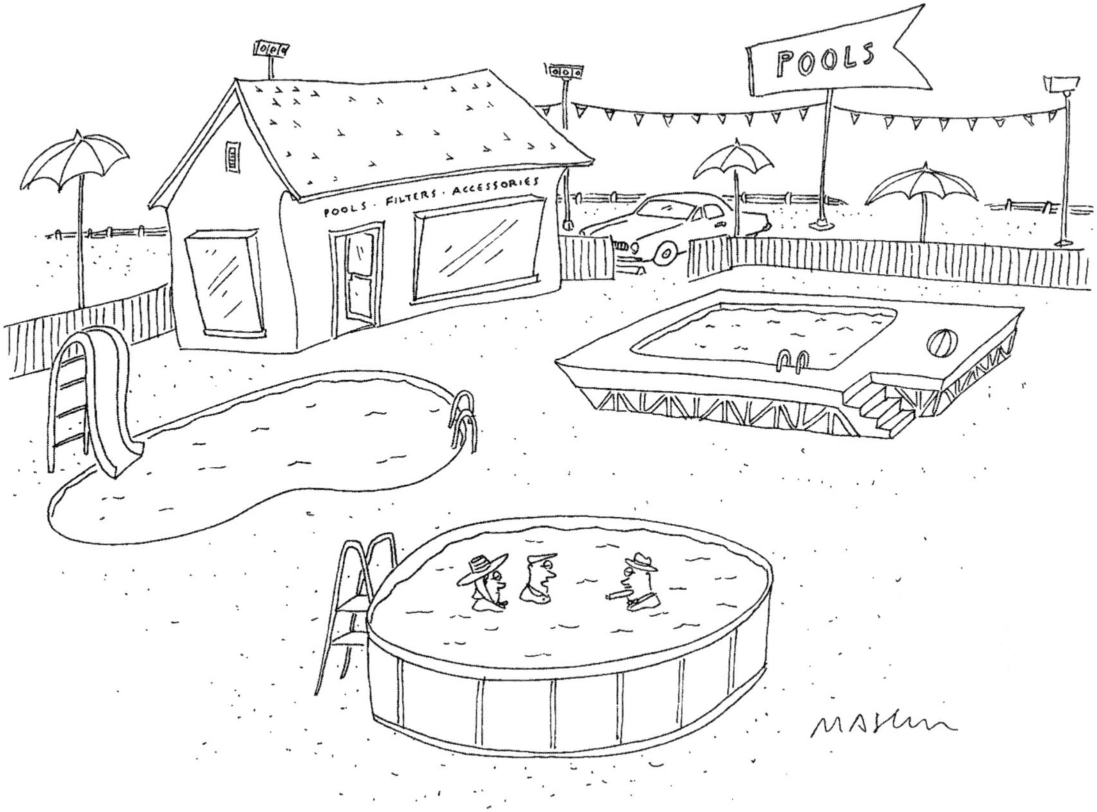
POOLS
POOLS · FILTERS · ACCESSORIES
MASLIN

"We'll take it."

"Your feet will certainly be happy
if it rains."

"Lately he's been spending more and more of his time with bell peppers
and less and less of his time with me."

"I wish we had tiptoed, not jumped, into wicker."

"He's more decorative than functional."

"In our first year of marriage we exposed our beams, too."

"That's New York. We wanted an apartment with a view of Chicago."

"If you don't up and run you'll finally get to meet my husband."

"If they're not your relatives and
they're not my relatives, whose relatives are they?"

Acknowledgments

We would like to thank our agent, David Kuhn, and our editor at Random House, Susan Mercandetti, for their encouragement and help in guiding us forward with this book. Thanks also to Billy Kingsland, Abigail Plesser, and Merrideth Miller for their expert assistance. Thanks as well to *The New Yorker*'s cartoon editor, Bob Mankoff, for his support.

Last, we wish to thank our matchmaker, *The New Yorker* magazine.

About the Authors

LIZA DONNELLY was born in Washington, D.C. A contract cartoonist with *The New Yorker,* Liza has been working for the magazine and many other national publications for over twenty years. Her book *Funny Ladies: The New Yorker's Greatest Women Cartoonists and Their Cartoons* is considered a must-have for fans and historians of the magazine. In 2008, she conceived of and edited a collection of cartoons, *Sex and Sensibility: Ten Women Examine the Lunacy of Modern Love . . . in 200 Cartoons.* She has also written and illustrated seven children's books. Liza is on the faculty of Vassar College in the Women's Studies and American Culture departments and frequently gives talks on cartooning, *The New Yorker,* and women's issues. Donnelly is a member of PEN and the Authors Guild. She is one of the original participants in the Cartooning for Peace initiative, which began in 2006 at the United Nations and continues worldwide.

MICHAEL MASLIN was born in Montclair, New Jersey, in 1953. He graduated from the University of Connecticut in 1976 and began contributing to *The New Yorker* in 1977, where he has been a contract artist since 1982. Four collections of his work have been published, in addition to one collection he coedited with Liza Donnelly and two collections they coauthored.

Donnelly and Maslin live in New York with their two daughters.

About the Type

This book was set in Gill Sans, a typeface designed by Eric Gill (1882–1940), a renowned writer, sculptor, wood engraver, book illustrator, and stonecutter, for the Monotype Corporation and released in 1929. Modeled on Edward Johnston's London Underground alphabet, Gill Sans is one of the few sans serif typefaces based on classical proportions, with idiosyncratic details that make it one of the most readable of those designed in the early twentieth century.